Ride The Wild Tiger

Ruth Tearle

comPress

First published in 2000 by comPress
www.compress.co.za
info@compress.co.za

Change Designs
www.changedesigns.co.za
info@changedesigns.co.za

ISBN 1-919833-09-9

Cover design by Graham Arbuckle
Author's photograph by Dirk Visser

Printed by Creda Communications, Epping

About the author

Ruth Tearle is the founder of Change Designs, a management consultancy specialising in strategic planning and change management. Change Designs provides facilitation, tools, research and structured activities which helps teams to create their own strategic plan, and to manage the transformation needed to achieve their vision. Change Design's website can be found at URL www.changedesigns.co.za. Ruth is also the author of *Managing Transition.*

Acknowledgements

To my husband Mike
— *the wind beneath my wings*

Thanks to all my clients, colleagues and friends who shared their stories with me, and encouraged me to write. To my editors Ross Frylinck and François van Schalkwyk of comPress whose dedication and creativity transformed my manuscript into this book.

Prologue

Life is like a wild tiger
you can either lie down
and let it lay its paw upon your head
or sit on its back and ride it
Ride the wild tiger

As we begin the twenty first century, more and more people are throwing off the reins of societal expectations and choosing instead, to ride the wild tiger.

Rather than waiting for long service awards, employees at all levels are taking charge of their lives. Some are resigning from top paying jobs in large corporations to find personal meaning outside of the corporation. Others are starting up businesses based on their personal dreams or embarking on adventures in newly developing countries.

Organisations are also learning to ride the wild tiger. Many are dissatisfied with the change programmes they have brought into their organisations. Downsizing, rightsizing, quality, business process reengineering, mass customisation, strategy, values, and customer care programmes seem to lack something. Something bold. Something meaningful. Something almost spiritual.

Those individuals and corporations who live by their

own rules have made a courageous change. A change as great as changing from a horse jockey to a rider of wild tigers.

What is the key difference between a horse and a tiger?

The difference lies in the nature of 'control'. You can control a horse. Bridles, saddles and whips can be used to tame the spirit of a wild horse. To 'break it in' so that it can be used by man.

In eastern literature, a tiger symbolises life, nature, guide, spirit, strength, courage, and uncontrolled power. A wild tiger can never be tamed. A man trying to control a tiger through force would only serve to enrage or kill the beast. However the literature also shows many examples of wild tigers carrying men on their backs. Harmony, rather than force is needed to ride the wild tiger.

But what if the world we are used to working in changes from horse to tiger territory? How do we become wild tiger riders? And how do we transform our organisations?

The book you are about to read is not a text book providing models of how to transform your organisation. Rather it is a story in which the hero, a typical corporate leader, embarks on a journey of self-discovery which takes him from first world America, to vibrant South Africa. With the help of certain insights, he discovers his personal wild tiger. He learns slowly and painfully to use this wisdom to create a wonderful organisation. An organisation filled with wild tiger riders.

1 *Horse Riding in Tiger Territory*

You were once wild here.
Don't let them tame you!

— Isadora Duncan

"But you're always too tired to play."

The arrow found a chink in Bill's shield of indifference. He kept silent, but the barb hurt. Yes he knew it was true. He was always tired. When he came home from work he longed to sink into a tranquil cocoon. Instead, he faced a boisterous fourteen year old who just wanted his attention. But how could he explain to his disappointed son that he just didn't have the energy. He just needed to be left alone.

Bill sank gratefully into the couch as Sharon gently steered Brad out of the room. As the strains of Bach filled the lounge, Bill felt the tension easing out of him. The music stopped abruptly. Sharon stood in front of him.

"You know," she said calmly, "children grow up so fast. In a few years time Brad will be an adult. I know you are under pressure at work, but it's time you got your life into balance. You are missing out on your son's childhood. If you're not careful, when you finally have time for your son, he won't have time for you. Think about it." With that, she left the room.

He sighed. It had been quite a week. He'd better try to give Brad some time. He dragged his body onto his feet and began walking slowly to the door. He felt awful. His eye caught his reflection in the hallway mirror. He stopped in surprise. An apparition with lifeless puffy eyes and a pasty skin was staring back at him. It couldn't possibly be him. He looked again. This time he noticed the black rings around his eyes. Where did these come from? He leaned closer to the mirror and examined his red hair. It had turned blond. No, it was grey and thinning at the temples. He straightened up to his full six foot and an half inch. He pulled in his abdomen and looked carefully down. A ring of blubber confirmed his worst suspicions. He grabbed his belly to verify the truth. A wave of self-disgust washed over him. It couldn't be true. He was only 43. He was disciplined. He never ate dessert. In fact he rarely had time to eat a full meal.

He felt absolutely drained. He couldn't cope with a diet right now. He wasn't even sure he could face Brad. Or anyone else. He desperately wanted, no needed, some space.

Sharon watched Bill pretending to be interested in Brad's Grand Prix computer game. The irritation welled up in her chest. 'I don't know why he even bothers,' she thought. 'He spends so little time with Brad, and when he eventually does, he may as well not be there. Everything seems like such an effort to him. Everything except work. He's always got energy for that. I bet you he's thinking about work right now. He is so obsessed with his job, nothing else matters to him any more. If Brad and I were to disappear right now, he probably wouldn't even notice. Is this how it has always been?' she thought bitterly. 'Is this all I have to look forward to for the rest of my life?'

An image floated into her mind of the day she'd met Bill. She'd been jogging in the park with her friend Pat, when a cheery voice had said, "Can I join you ladies if I promise to try to keep up?" Pat had punched her brother on the shoulder. "You're only prepared to run with me when I'm with Sharon," she'd complained. "Exactly," he teased. I can only do my John Cleese routine before an appreciative audience." At that he slowed his pace down to theirs, leaping from one foot to the other. He'd looked ridiculous and they'd all laughed. And that was Bill, full of fun, energy and mischief. An easy man to fall in love with. Sharon recalled the early days of their marriage. A time brimming with laughter, adventure, and love. Images floated into her memory of a special week of windsurfing, hiking, an outdoor symphony concert and a surprise picnic. That was when Brad had been conceived.

Her eyes fixed on the dark-souled man before her. Who was this gloomy, irritable man burdened by a yoke of responsibility? What had happened to the carefree Bill she'd adored?

She watched as Brad expertly manoeuvred the Ferrari around the track. He pulled the stick down and

Schumacher zoomed passed the checkered flag. The Tifosi fans roared. Brad grinned. "Everyone loves Ferrari. Your turn Dad, or should I say "Mika Hakkinen."

The cars lined up on the track. The lights turned green and away they went. Hakkinen in his Mercedes Mclaren accelerated down the straight. "Slow down Dad!" yelled Brad as the car hit the corner and skidded onto the sand-bank. Bill cursed and manoeuvred the car back onto the track. He pulled down the joystick, the Mclaren surged forward, collided with the barrier and swung around. "Watch out for the tail enders," shouted Brad. Too late. With a crash and a bang, Hakkinen was out of the race.

"You were really awful, Dad!" exclaimed Brad. "You've gotta slow down. Otherwise you'll just keep on crashing."

"That's the story of my life," muttered Bill.

'It's all part of the same pattern. You push too hard at work and then crash at home. I'm getting tired of picking up the pieces,' the shrew inside Sharon whispered.

"Dinner will be ready in 20 minutes", said the adult Sharon whilst strangling her dark shadow.

Bill slunk back to the lounge. He sighed. 'Some space at last.' The phone rang insistently. "I'm not here," shouted Bill.

Sharon persisted. "It's Phil asking if you want a game of racquet ball."

"I told you I'm not here," Bill cried in exasperation.

He heard Sharon chatting in the background. She appeared irritated. "I can't keep making excuses for you. They're your friends, not mine. And it's time you exercised your body anyway."

A wall of tension descended, stifling Bill. He sighed again. No one understood how he felt. He just couldn't cope with the incessant demands anymore. Everyone wanted a chunk of him and he had nothing left to give. All he wanted was half an hour alone with no demands on him. Was that too much to ask for? It seemed like every second of his life was being consumed by a flock of vultures, and he could no longer fight them off. Meetings with staff, reports for the boss and workshops with consultants crammed his days. And his evenings were filled with more demands from Sharon, Brad, his parents, his sister and now even his friends. He didn't even have time to listen to music, let alone do what the card suggested...

He picked up the card he'd found in his in-tray that day and read the words:

Every day nature paints a sunset, whether you're there to appreciate it, or not.

He examined the card. The size of a credit card, light purple in colour, it was smudged and dog-eared. On the front was a diagram of a tiger and the words 'Ride the wild tiger'. At the bottom of the card was what looked like an address. It was badly smudged. He couldn't quite make it out, but it looked like an address had been deliberately scratched out.

"Hmmf!" he snorted. "I can't even get five minutes to

myself to listen to music. When on earth would I find time to watch a sunset?" A cloud of sadness enveloped him. A wave of cynicism washed it away. "I wonder which joker sent me that card and why?"

He leant back in his chair. He felt so weary. "I just wish I had the energy to see the sunsets, play with my son, be a good husband and friend," he thought. "But I don't." Why couldn't his family and friends understand the pressure he was under? He felt he'd spent the last year running a marathon through a bog of treacle. He was exhausted and had nothing left to give.

Had he always been tired? His mind drifted through the five years that he'd been running Papas. During the first few years he'd been full of energy. He'd played racquet ball three times a week, had studied an MBA part time, and had succeeded in transforming Papas from a loss maker into the most profitable group of stores in the DollarMart chain.

When he took over as CEO, Papas had consisted of three retail stores which sold clothing and shoes to farmers and their workers in the South. The company was losing $1.2m per annum. Within three years Papas had expanded to a chain of sixteen stores and a mail order business which sold clothing, shoes and accessories to middle class males and females throughout the state. Annual profits increased to $16m. Head office was smiling. So was his management team. It had taken a lot out of them all to manage the expansion, but they'd pulled together, and achieved what everyone else said was impossible to do. By 1996, Papas had 22% of the market share for clothing and accessories in the state. Bill felt justifiably proud of this achievement. But what pleased him most of all, was the powerful management team he'd been able to develop in the process. Papas was being led by a team of go-getters and achievers. And he felt a private sense of pride in managing to graduate with his part-time MBA. Those were good times.

When had it all gone wrong? His memory flicked through image after image, stopping on the day he'd first met Chuck Anderson. He remembered coming back from lunch and seeing this kid sitting in his office. Chuck, with his unkempt hair, a pale pimpled face, badly creased jeans and dirty sneakers, had looked so out of place in an office.

At first he'd been gentle with the gangly 23 year old computer science dropout who had arrived without an appointment. He had just wanted to tell Bill about 'this wild business idea' he'd had 'that might just fly'. The youngster, who had no work experience, qualifications or capital had set up a website called FASH@US to sell clothing and accessories via the Internet. His reason for approaching Papas was to secure an established distribution system in the South.

Bill had been amused by Chuck's impudence. The kid was barely out of school and already wanting to run the show. What did Chuck know about retail? What did he understand about merchandising? He obviously hadn't done any market research. Didn't he know that Papas' target market wasn't interested in computers? The last survey showed that his customers wanted human interaction and personal service. Papas had spent three years building a reputation for caring, personalised service and the market had responded. A 22% market share proved that his strategy was correct. Now a 23 year-old IT dropout wanted Papas to become his distribution system. This kid had some nerve. He'd obviously shown Chuck the door.

His mind began sifting through the memories of the next six months. He recalled watching Brad admiring himself in the mirror.

"Nice pair of jeans," he'd said to Brad. "Where did you get them?"

"From Owens," enthused Brad. Bill looked puzzled. Owens was one of Papas' smaller and duller competitors. Why on earth would a fashion conscious kid like Brad shop at Owens?

"You should go to Owens yourself, Dad" said Brad. "It's really cool there. They have this neat touch screen computer which allows you to surf inside a virtual shopping mall. You choose the shop you want to visit, and suddenly you're inside the store. They have all these different designs of jeans hanging on racks. You can look at each pair in detail on the screen, or you can choose to see a model of your choice wearing the jeans. I chose Brad Pitt to model my jeans. Then I chose Cindy Crawford. Ooh la la!" Brad looked at his father who appeared concerned. "Don't worry dad, she had a T-shirt on!"

"Anyway, after that I just had to key in my size and

colour preference and specify how I'd be paying. Then I pressed 'Send'. Three days later Owens phoned to say they'd got my jeans. And do you know what… Owens says they are going to install some more of these touch screens at our school next year."

Bill was concerned. If Chuck could hook Brad, then he was a threat. Next month Papas' market share had dropped two points. Bill immediately called a meeting of his senior management team to discuss ways of reducing the novelty threat of the Internet on their teenage market. His team rose to the challenge. They code named their strategy 'The Teen Challenge'. The whole company galvanised around the cause. Papas' buyers searched the globe for new and exciting teen merchandise. Marketing planned mind-blowing promotions and competitions. Celebrities visited the stores. Papas featured in all the teen magazines, and competitions with exciting prizes lured the teenagers back to the store.

Bill looked at the sales figures that month and relaxed. Market share had risen by three points. He was right to have confidence in his team. Once again they'd met a challenge head on and pulled through together. He was proud of them all.

The dinner party Bill and Sharon attended a few months later was not teen stuff. Their hostess Jane, a real social butterfly, was wearing a stunning black cocktail dress that framed her carefully highlighted blonde hair. Something inside Bill made him act out of character and ask Jane where she's bought her dress. Bill wasn't even surprised by her answer.

"From Owens," remarked Jane casually. "No, it wasn't actually from Owens. I chose it at our local bookstore and collected it from Owens." She paused, waiting for a reaction.

Sharon provided it "Are you saying that you ordered a dress from a bookstore?"

Jane was in her element. She continued. "You know how much time I spend at Bookdelight. Well they have this amazing little coffee shop inside the book-store where you can relax and read your magazines. Last week they developed a new section in the coffee shop called 'The Internet Cafe.' The manager of the store knows me very well. She insisted that I surf the Internet. When I told her what a technophobe I was, she told me all you need to know about using the Net is your credit card number."

They all smiled. They knew about Jane and her credit card. She laughed.

"My credit card number is the one thing I do know. So I agreed. With the click of a mouse, I was inside this incredible virtual shopping mall. There were departmental stores, shoe shops, boutiques, sports stores, travel agents and hundreds of other exciting shops to choose from. The manager left me alone, and I went into a number of stores. It was amazing. I finally found a designer boutique that blew my mind.

Imagine this Sharon. You begin by choosing the type of clothing you are interested in. You have a choice of eveningwear, power dressing, casualwear or sports gear. I chose eveningwear. I then browsed through a book containing the original artwork by the actual designers. When I found a design I liked, I had a choice of viewing it in the colour and length I wanted. I then keyed in my measurements, hair colour and skin tone and was able to view it on a model who looked quite similar to me. I was hooked. I ordered the dress I'm wearing now, right there and then. The hardest thing about using the Internet was to choose between paying by credit card and having the manufacturer deliver my dress via Federal Express to my home, or paying by cash and collecting the dress from one of 20 retail stores in my area. Now don't laugh. I chose the cash option and collected from Owens because I didn't want to have to stay at home waiting for a delivery, and Owens is so convenient. So I didn't even have to use my credit card after all."

Everyone laughed. Except Bill. "But I thought that you once said that Owens was a tacky store, and you'd never be seen dead inside it," observed Bill.

"I did," agreed Jane. "But I didn't actually go inside the store. I simply collected a parcel from their front desk."

Bill refused to give up. "But what about personal service?" he demanded. "I thought that you once said that that was why you only shop at Macy's. Aren't you being a bit fickle?"

Jane took the bait, but not in the way Bill expected.

"You want to talk about service?" Jane retorted. "This Internet thing has it right. Think about it. I don't have to try on hundreds of outfits only to be told that the size that I want isn't in stock. Or that they have run out of my colour. But maybe their other branch might have what I am looking for. I don't have to listen to some silly shop assistant trying to convince me that I look stunning in an outfit three sizes too small for me and a colour that makes me look ill. You call that personal service? At Bookdelight I can sit comfortably and order exactly what I want over a cup of coffee. That's far more civilised, wouldn't you say?"

Bill touched his neck. It felt cold. He turned to Arnie who manufactured sports clothing. "What do you think of the Internet, Arnie?"

Arnie's response did not reassure Bill. "It's interesting you should ask that. We're currently working on a trial project with a chap called Chuck Anderson. At the moment, we are using the Internet as a way of getting rid of our excess stock. For a few hundred dollars we are represented on Chuck's virtual shopping mall. Customers order what they want from the website. Chuck arranged a special deal with Federal Express, who collect all our orders at 3 p.m. each day and charge us a reduced rate. They deliver to the customer the very next day, and Chuck transfers the amount owed to us electronically within 48 hours. It's good for our cash flow, and it's a great strategy. Not only are we getting rid of excess stock which is tying up our capital, but we're being paid for it within two days. We also look inexpensive to the end customer, as we're cutting out the middle man. Our company believes that this experiment has worked well, so we're meeting with Chuck next week to look at what else we should be marketing over the Internet."

The next morning, in the office, Jane's story kept on churning through Bill's head. Yes he was concerned. When someone like 'credit card Jane' enthused about a new shopping option, there was definitely something to worry about. And when Arnie's conservative company believed an experiment had worked well, then the strategy must be practically risk free.

Bill called a meeting of his team to discuss this potential threat. Bob, the marketing director, brought the latest sales figures. To Bill's surprise, the figures looked normal. After much debate the team decided that they needed more information about the threat before Papas changed its strategy. Bob undertook to hire an independent market research agency to survey Papas' target markets. Tom, the operations director, suggested that they confront the threat itself – the Internet. He undertook to do some research on the Internet to determine what it could and could not do, and how other companies were using it. Meanwhile the entire team agreed to constantly monitor the situation.

A few weeks later, Bill happened to bump into Owens himself on a street corner. He asked Owens why he, a retailer, had chosen to link up with Chuck Anderson.

"It's the best thing that ever happened to me," explained Owens. "I've found a way to carry minimal stock, offer greater variety, lower my cost structure and become 'cool' to teenagers in one easy stroke. And I'm now also appealing to the designer market."

As Owens spoke, Bill watched the wind swirl up the litter on the sidewalk and dump it unceremoniously in the street, under the wheels of an oncoming truck. He shuddered. Back at the office, Bill immediately asked for the latest market share statistics and for an update on the progress of the market research. This time the figures bore out his worst fears. Papas' market share had dropped to 15%. As he was analysing the situation, a call came through from head office. Roger, director of operations for the DollarMart group sounded concerned. "Bill, we've picked up a substantial drop in your market share statistics. What's happening?"

Bill felt defensive. He couldn't quite believe it. He'd barely read the figures himself and already his boss was on the phone. He noticed that Roger hadn't managed to find the time to congratulate him on the outstanding sales figures resulting from the 'Teen Challenge' campaign. But a simple slip in market share figures had him instantly on the phone.

"Don't worry Roger," he responded calmly. "We noticed the drop here too. We are conducting market research right now to determine if this is simply a blip on the radar screen, or something that requires a change of strategy. But we have it all under control."

Bill followed up on the progress of the market research. The Market Research America (MRA) was conducting a series of focus groups in Papas' target markets.

This methodology took longer than simple surveys, but yielded more detailed qualitative results. Bill could expect the final report in six weeks time. Bill was impatient; he knew that head office was expecting things to happen fast. He asked the market research company to provide him with an interim report.

On the day MRA was due to present its initial findings, Bill received the latest market share statistics. Papas was down by a further 7%. Suddenly everyone was keen to get an indication of the cause of their problems from MRA. Andy, the Accounts Executive at MRA warned that at this stage of the research, their data could not be validated. However, the research pointed to a number of key factors affecting the buying decisions of their target markets. These were 'quality, value for money, ambience, personal customer care, image and an enjoyable shopping experience.'

John, the accountant, voiced everyone's frustrations. "Are you telling us that after a month, this is all you've come up with? I could have told you this myself before you did the research. What we need to know is this: what does each target market mean by 'quality'? How does Papas rate on each of these factors? How do our competitors rate? How many people are shopping or intend shopping via the Internet? What does Papas need to do to achieve a competitive edge?"

Andy's disdainful reply didn't reassure the team. He proceeded to 'take the team through the methodology they were using,' and explained why this approach was required. He explained that answering the detailed questions required by John was not in the original brief, and therefore would take more time. Bill was disappointed. They had wasted an entire month, and had nothing to show for it. But there was nothing he could do right now. They had to wait for MRA to complete its research.

There was a message on his desk to phone Roger at head office. Bill sighed. What was he going to say to him? He knew their results didn't look good, but he decided that honesty was the best policy. He admitted to Roger that he too was concerned about the drop in market share, and that he'd just asked for an interim report from MRA to determine what was going on. Roger asked him to fax a copy of the report.

A few days later Bill received a call from Lisa Brown at head office. Lisa headed the DollarMart's Total Quality Management (TQM) division, and Roger had suggested she may be able to help Bill.

Bill recalled his first meeting with Lisa and Brian from TQM. Lisa entered the room first. Modelling a pinstriped navy suit, the 28 year old blonde graduate enthused Total Quality Management from every pore. Brian, who used to work for a large auditing firm, was more businesslike in his approach. Bill briefed the TQM team about what had happened since Chuck Anderson had launched his FASH@US website. He mentioned the loss in market share, the Teen Challenge campaign, and the further decline in market share.

Lisa looked thrilled "This is so exciting," she exclaimed.

"Papas is an ideal candidate for TQM."

"Yes," added Brian. "TQM will help Papas to build a 'sustainable competitive advantage' in its future markets. And with just a little time and commitment from you, you'll be amazed at the results you'll get from TQM." Their enthusiasm was infectious. The senior management team committed themselves to implementing TQM throughout Papas.

Bill was quite excited about what TQM could do for Papas. His team were less impressed. "Young, Harvard graduates with a mission" was Tom's description of them.

"Interference from head office," was how Bob saw them.

Bill explained that Roger had sent Lisa and Brian to Papas. The least they could do was to give it a try.

If only he'd known then how much time and energy TQM would consume. Bill closed his eyes. Hundreds of flipcharts with thousands of unsorted ideas danced before his eyes. He felt angry. This is what he'd got out of 32 workshops. Thirty-two days of having to open each workshop to demonstrate his commitment to the process. Sixty four hours in which he was put on the spot. He remembered Lisa's instructions of how he and his team had to listen carefully to all the ideas that emerged during the workshop. They would then have 10 minutes to decide which ideas should be implemented and which should be canned. He should have known then that this would become a no-win situation. If he'd given the go-ahead to implement some of these impractical ideas, Papas' staff would have diverted their focus away from their core business. On the other hand, if he'd said no to any idea, he and his team would have had to provide solid reasons as to why that idea could not be implemented, knowing that this would destroy the morale of the group. An impossible task.

That month they lost a further 3% market share. This time Roger insisted that Papas use Sue Eagle. Sue was an expert in Value Chain Analysis and Business Process Reengineering.

Tom called Sue the expert in Analysis Paralysis.

Sue wondered why Bill had gone with TQM, when Business Process Reengineering was what was required for a business problem such as his. Bill felt quite angry about the time he'd already spent. His team were less polite.

"We have a business to run. We can't keep wasting time on pointless workshops. We need to focus on rebuilding our market share." It was the first time there'd been conflict in his team.

Bill had phoned Roger. "These workshops don't seem to be helping us," he'd said. "In fact they are diverting our focus away from the real business. So we won't be using Sue."

Roger would have none of it. "Every division of DollarMart is going through a reengineering process, and Papas is no exception. If any division needs to reengineer, it's Papas. You have been under-performing for the last six months. I am giving you a direct order to co-operate with Sue."

So Bill and his team had once again gone along with the endless workshops, flipcharts, and brainstorming of ideas that didn't address the real issue.

Four months later, Papas' market share stood at 12%. The team that had once risen to any challenge was being smothered by uncooperative behaviour, conflict, and mountains of paper. Bill wondered how he was going to handle the situation with Tom. When he'd asked Tom for the latest sales figures, Tom had responded angrily with "I didn't have time to compile them". When Bill had asked him when he could expect to get the figures, Tom had muttered, "When you stop sending me on these stupid workshops".

The team then started arguing about the relevance of the Business Process Reengineering and TQM workshops to Papas. John commented, "Surely we should be focusing on our real problems, rather than the problems being dreamed up by consultants?"

Bill came home exhausted. All he wanted was some space to work out what to do. But then Brad wanted his attention. And Sharon. How could he explain to them that nothing was working for him anymore. That Papas' sales and market share statistics kept falling no matter what he did. That the management team he'd been so proud of was now spending their time bickering with one another. And how was he going to tell Roger that he wasn't going to waste any more time doing these workshops.

Bill sighed yet again. Sharon exploded:"I wish you'd stop sighing all the time, and get off your butt and help around the house. You come home night after night, moping about all your work problems; do you think you're the only one that has problems at work?"

Bill couldn't believe what he'd just heard. He didn't have the energy to respond. Just when he needed Sharon's support the most, she'd started attacking him. They ate dinner in silence.

Bill didn't sleep all night. By the next morning he'd worked out what he was going to do. He was going to call his team together, and develop a new strategy for dealing with the current situation. Then he was going to call Roger and tell him not to send any more consultants. Bill's team was going to restore Papas' market share their way – just like they'd done before.

As he entered the office his secretary told him that Roger had booked a meeting with him at 10 O'clock.

"Great timing," he thought. "Just when I wanted to see him." Roger's secretary showed Bill into his office. Bill at once noticed Roger's desk. A solitary sheet of paper decorated the wooden desk. As Bill walked in, Roger finished signing the paper and handed it to Amanda. Bill wondered how he could be so organised.

"I'm pleased you arranged this meeting, as I've been doing some thinking about how to restore Papas' market share," began Bill. Roger heard him out.

Then he stood up, and perched on the edge of the desk. His words fired like bullets from a machine gun;

"I'm sorry Bill, but we can't carry on like this any longer. You don't seem to be in control any longer. You're not achieving your targets. You lose your temper at the slightest thing, and you're always stressed and irritable. We don't believe you have what it takes to lead Papas into the next century. Sorry Bill, but you'll have to go. Amanda has the papers for you to sign."

2 Shoot the Crippled Horse

It doesn't matter if the water is cold or warm if you're going to have to wade through it anyway

— Teilhard De Chardin

"They can't do this to me! After all I've given them! After all I've done for them! If it wasn't for me, Papas would still be a two-bit company. I'm the one that built up the business from six to twenty two stores. I developed the leadership team. I turned the company around and made it what it is today. They can't do this to me. There must be some mistake. I bet you Ted, the managing director isn't even aware of what Roger has done."

Sharon listened silently to Bill's tirade. She felt so sorry for Bill. Papas had been his life for six years. He'd given everything to the company. He didn't deserve this. Yet a small part of her was secretly pleased at what this meant to her and to Brad. Her workaholic husband had been torn away from his obsession. Maybe when all the pain had subsided, the Bill she'd fallen in love with would come bouncing back. She watched Bill pick up the phone.

"Ted Blewitt please," she heard him say. "I'd like to come and see you to discuss what is happening at Papas."

He waited nervously. She heard him say "Yes, yes," and "but." She watched his body crumple as the force of Ted's words hit him. He put the phone down and looked at her in disbelief.

"He says not to come in. He knew about what Roger was going to do from the start. He says it's over."

He looked so small and vulnerable. Sharon went over and hugged him. He held her desperately. "It's just not fair," he sobbed. "I know. I know," was all she could say.

For the next few weeks, Bill kept in touch with what was happening at Papas. Sharon shared her concerns with Pat, Bill's sister. "I don't know what to do. He keeps contacting everyone at work. He can't let go. I think he's becoming a pest to them, but they're just too polite to tell him. Everyday Bill informs me about the latest betrayals."

"Like what?" asked Pat.

Sharon dropped her voice and mimicked Bill: "Peter from IT reckons the company made a big mistake in firing me. Market share has dropped even lower and the share price has dived since I left. Shelly from PR said that Tom has taken over as MD. Can you believe that. If it wasn't for me, he'd be a junior accounting officer today. How could he do this to me?"

Pat listened carefully. "Sounds like denial," she observed.

Sharon continued, "Adrian from operations has said that the company has announced it is getting rid of all the consultants and is going back to basics. That's just what I was going to do when they fired me. Adrian also told me that Roger accused me of being responsible for bringing all the consultants into the firm. How can he say that when he knows that he was the one that foisted Lisa, Brian and Sue onto me when I didn't want them. I had everything under control..."

"Uh Uh," sympathised Pat. My poor brother is hurting badly. He's going to go through a rough time. And he's going to need a lot of support."

"I know," sighed Sharon. "I just wish it were all over. He's not even thinking of finding a new job, and I'm not sure how we're going to cope on my salary." That night, Sharon tried to mention her concerns to Bill.

"Don't worry about it," snapped Bill. "I'm going to collect my severance cheque from Papas tomorrow. I'll cash in my share options; we'll have plenty to live on until I find another job."

He arrived home that afternoon looking pale and shaking with anger.

"What happened?" she asked.

"They've given me a month's notice and that's all." He looked scared.

"But they can't do that?" questioned Sharon. "What about all the share options?"

"They say that since I was fired, I'm not entitled to anything."

"What are you going to do?" she asked.

"I don't know." he wimpered.

At the barbecue evening at his sister's, Bill had it all worked out. "I'm going to hire a lawyer," he told Pat's husband." I'm going to sue them for every cent due to me."

"I don't know if it's such a good idea," remarked Pat. "They could string out the court case for years, bankrupting you in the process."

Bill exploded: "These big corporates think they can treat people like dirt, and get away with it. They count on the little guy being too scared to fight back. Well this time they've chosen the wrong person. I'll do whatever it takes!"

"Well," said the ever practical Pat, "if you're going to go through it, you'd better use Pete's lawyer. Apparently they work on a fixed fee upfront, and then a share of whatever you win. At least you can control your risk." She handed him a card.

The following week Bill arrived for his appointment at the legal firm Hoffman, Kramer and Fisher. While waiting for Bruce McNamee, the firm's expert on company and labour law, Bill gazed at the marbelled floors, the teak furniture, and the designer-dressed receptionist. He shuddered involuntarily. What if he lost the case and was stuck with these sort of fees? Bruce McNamee reassured him at once. Peter had phoned him to explain Bill's situation. They would limit his exposure. He asked Bill to tell him what had happened.

"So?" asked Sharon, "What happened? What did he say?"

"He said he thought we had a good case."

"And..." She insisted.

"Well I can pay a fixed fee. After that, he'll take a percentage of the settlement. So at least I'm not going to be risking everything."

Jane and Arnie demanded more details over dinner. And Bill, the centre of attention, obliged.

"I told Bruce how I'd built up Papas, how Roger foisted consultants onto me, and how he expected me to take the blame when their strategies didn't work out. He took a lot of notes. Then he asked me to collect any documentation I can get my hands on such as letters of appointment, company policies and so on. I'm seeing him next week for another appointment. And then we'll going to nail Roger for what he did to me..."

"What was Bruce like? Was he a hunk?" Sharon was pleased that Jane had asked the question. She also wanted to know more about the man who was going to make her husband feel good about himself again. She heard her reticent husband describing a 33 year old who wore Armani suits. A professional who cared about what was happening to Bill. A man who believed in going after what was 'only fair'. A competent attorney who'd have this whole thing over and done with within a month.

One month expanded into three and then into six. Pat was concerned about her brother. He seemed trapped in a vicious cycle of revenge and humiliation. Every time Bill had to fly up to New York to see the DollarMart's legal representative, he came back a little emptier, less confident, and more obsessed with revenge. She wished he could end it all. But like a gambler on a losing streak, he simply couldn't stop. She felt torn between her friend Sharon, and her brother, both of whom were suffering in their own ways.

Sharon found herself becoming increasingly irritable. For the first time in her life she looked and felt old. She couldn't understand why she had no energy. Why couldn't she sleep at night? Why did she snap angrily at Bill when she was trying so hard to be supportive? She was working overtime to pay off the debts they were accumulating. She tried to protect Bill from routine household problems. She explained to Brad that his father was not ignoring him, but was immersed in problems he needed to focus on. The weight of all the responsibility was exhausting her. She wished she could share it, but Bill was always too busy preparing his case, or complaining about how unfair Papas had been to him.

One day the mounting frustration exploded. "Everything has to revolve around you and your pride. 'Poor Bill.' The world is always treating you so badly. It's time you stopped being selfish and considered how you're affecting those around you. Look at Brad. He's too scared to say two words to you in case you lose your temper or go into depression. And you, you're too busy preparing for a case that is never going to be won, to do anything else. I'm having to shoulder all the responsibility around here. I'm the only breadwinner now. Yet I still have to come home to cook, clean and support you. The least you could do is to help around the house!"

Sharon saw the hurt in Bill's face and felt awful. She

hadn't meant to say it, but the words had slipped out. It's not my fault, she rationalised to herself. He's become totally obsessed. They offered him a settlement five months ago, which I begged him to take. But no, he was too proud. $50,000 was an 'insult'. He had to fight 'on principle'. God I hate people who are so fixated on principles, that they can't see reality. "Why should they get away with it?" he'd complained. So he had to fight for what was 'rightfully his'. They crushed him. They told him he'd been a lousy manager and offered him $20,000. He still couldn't take it 'on principle'. She sighed. How much longer was he going to take to get the message. He had to let go of his obsession with Papas and get on with his life.

Bill was hurt by Sharon's attack. "You're the one person I thought I could count on," he thought. He wondered if he should give up the fight. That would mean letting Papas win after all.

He'd really believed he'd come out with at least $100,000. Now the most he could expect was $20,000. It simply wasn't fair. At the first meeting it seemed like everything was going to be all right. Roger and Ted had expressed their regret for what had happened. Bill's heart had soared. Maybe they were going to admit their error and hire him back. But then they'd offered him $50,000 for an immediate settlement. He'd considered that to be an insult and told them so. After all, he'd given Papas six years of his life. He'd built the damn business, and he expected some loyalty in return. Roger said Papas had tabled a fair offer and that Bill should reflect on it."

With hindsight he should have accepted their offer. But at the time, he couldn't believe that they were going to get away with unjustly firing him, and then depriving him of all the share options he'd been entitled to. It was wrong. It was insulting. He simply couldn't accept it. So he'd asked Bruce to set up another meeting with a counter offer of $75,000.

He remembered how angry he'd been when they'd purposely kept him and Bruce waiting for an hour. They didn't even offer them coffee at the meeting. They began by stating that they were withdrawing their previous offer of $50,000. Before he could say another word, they handed Bruce a list of actions Bill had failed to comply with as CEO. In view of this, they believed they didn't owe him a cent. He remembered grabbing the list from Bruce. Something inside him exploded. They accused him of failing to provide DollarMart with weekly reports as requested. But Roger had insisted he only required them monthly. They showed how Bill had managed to reduce Papas' market share from 24% to 12%. They ignored the fact that he'd been the one who'd built up the business in the first place. They accused him of being distracted by workshops, claimed he'd failed to take the necessary action to save their market share. The emotions welled up inside Bill and oozed out. Anger, hurt, frustration and humiliation infected his every word. "I wonder how you can sit there with such self righteous looks on your faces. You can't take responsibility for forcing those stupid workshops down my throat. Now you're trying to use me as a scapegoat for your own mistakes. I wonder how you can sleep at night," he'd shouted. He'd got up and walked out.

They had set up another meeting in which they'd hoped to make a final settlement. As Bill and Bruce were about to check in for their flight they received a call saying the meeting had to be cancelled. Bill was furious. "I don't believe they can be so rude," he fumed. "Just negotiating tactics," observed Bruce.

The next day Bruce called Bill to his office. "I'm wondering if it would be wise to continue with this case?"

"Why are you asking me this?" Bill folded his arms defensively.

"Because," cautioned Bruce, "they're starting to play ugly. You could get hurt."

"How much more can they hurt me?" demanded Bill. "They've already taken away my job, my money and my pride. What more can they take away?"

Bruce stared thoughtfully at Bill. He hesitated; then reluctantly he passed Bill a wad of papers.

"I'm going to leave the room now. Read these at your leisure and take some time to think about what you want to do."

Bill sat still. He summoned up his courage and read the covering letter. His team had written affidavits about him. A cloud of apprehension enveloped him. He scanned the opening lines. "I have worked for Bill for six years..." He skimmed through the lines until he read, "He never fully understood what it took to run a business". The blow winded him. He couldn't breathe. He grabbed the next sheet. What would John say? The lines blurred until one sentence came into focus. "Bill couldn't make a decision on his own. His lack of guts resulted in the company losing 12% of their market within six months." He flipped urgently through the remaining pages – searching for someone he could trust. He grabbed the affidavit from his friend Peter. Peter would surely tell the truth. He scanned through the legalese and read "Bill was a weak leader – unpopular with his team". He felt the tears prickling his eyes and wiped them away. He took a deep breath and began again. He carefully re-read each affidavit. When he'd finished he sat still for what seemed like ages. Then he slowly rose, gathered the papers and walked out in a daze. What should he do? He couldn't go home. Not now. He would walk. If he just kept walking he'd be ok.

He felt strangely disconnected. It was almost as though there were two Bills competing for his mind. The Bill he knew was wounded. Immobilised by pain. The Bill who couldn't believe how unfair the world was. Everyone seemed to be against him. Rob, Ted, Sharon, and now his team. He'd given his life to them all, and they, ungrateful lot, were throwing it back at him. No one cared about him at all.

But another voice, from somewhere deep inside, kept popping up. "It's only your pride that's been hurt. That's all." He stopped walking. It was true. He had put his pride in his team. His self-esteem had been tied to his job. And now that was gone, there was nothing left. What was he going to do? Should he stop fighting and let Papas win? Should he allow them to get away with the way they'd treated him?

His foot kicked against something. It hurt. He looked down to see what had caused the pain. It was a brick in the middle of the pathway. He was about to move it out of harms way when he noticed something purple sticking out. He bent down and picked up the laminated card. Yes, he was right. There was a tiger on the front. He turned it over in anticipation.

It makes no difference
if it's fair,
or not.

He looked at the card in awe. Then he found himself laughing. It was amazing how true this card was. No one cared anymore about right or wrong. About what was fair or not. His fighting would make no difference to the end result. Papas was going to get away with it after all.

The bag of depression dropped from his shoulders. He didn't have to fight anymore. He was going to ask the lawyer to get him the best deal possible. Whatever that was, he'd accept it.

He came home and told Sharon that he was going to stop fighting. He noticed the tears in her eyes. "Are you sure that's what you want to do?" she asked. He nodded.

He didn't want to fly to New York for the last meeting.

He was weary. His body ached. He wondered if he was catching flu. He steeled himself with the thought that he just had to get through one more day. Eight more hours and it would be all over. They were flying home at 5 O'clock. By 7 O'clock he could be in bed.

They arrived at Dollarmart's office in time for the 1pm meeting. As they waited for Roger and Ted, he felt his headache worsening. He took some headache pills. Where was Roger? It was now 1.30 p.m. Roger's secretary buzzed in and announced that Mr Templeton had been delayed, and would they mind waiting a little longer. It was now 2.30 p.m.

"What could be so important to Roger that he would be this rude?" muttered Bill. Even Bruce was looking irritated. The phone rang. "Mr Templeton is attending to a crisis. He won't be much longer," sang the cheery receptionist.

Bill looked at his watch, which showed 2.45 p.m. His heart sunk. He couldn't go through this again. They had to have this meeting today, and time was running out. They would have to leave for the airport at 3.30 p.m. if they were going to catch their plane. And Roger knew it, the bastard. Bruce wanted to get up and go, but Bill pleaded with him. "Let's just finish it off. No matter how rude they are."

At 3.10 p.m Roger breezed in. Without pausing to apologise he led them into the conference room. "Right," he said "Our final offer is $30,000."

"I'll take it."

Bruce grabbed the paperwork. Bill signed each sheet. They rushed out of the office to catch the plane.

As the plane began its descent to Atlanta, Bruce commented, "Keeping us waiting till we had only half an hour to go is an old negotiating trick. You could have held out for more, you know."

"I know," said Bill. "Thanks for what you've done."

He didn't remember how he got home that night. His last thoughts as he sank into his bed were: 'I've survived the day. The nightmare is finally over.' As he drifted off, a final idea glowed in his mind... 'I am free'.

3 A Fresh Horse To Nowhere

Not until we are lost do we begin to understand ourselves

— Henry David Thoreau

"So, what are you going to do now?" asked Arnie.

"I'm being kept busy all the time," replied Bill. "I'm getting in touch with all my old contacts. People I haven't seen for years. It's great to catch up with them again. Last Wednesday I networked with my old friend Beryl, who is the marketing director of Macy's. She thinks they may have something going in their merchandising department. On Friday I had lunch with Di from Avis. She tells me they're looking for an operations manager for their airport branch. On Monday I'm seeing a chap from Sportsman's Warehouse. Wednesday I've got an appointment with a contact in Starbucks. I might even open up a franchise. How'd you like to have a cappuccino and muffin after a hectic day of shopping, Jane" he teased.

"After shopping? If you want to compete with Bookdelight, you'd better provide me with Internet access so I can drink my coffee while I'm shopping," retorted Jane.

They all laughed. Bill thought back to how much he had learned about the Internet in the month since he left Papas. "Did you know I'm now an Internet fan too? Brad has been teaching me how to use the Internet. It has opened up a whole new world for me. I can tour the entire globe in a few hours, shop for anything, read the latest news bulletins, and check out the baseball scores. I can even see what's available on the job market via 'Jobs Online', and with e-mail, I don't even have to bother printing out my CV and posting it. I've already e-mailed my CV to eight companies and have had two responses. Brad is now even trying to get me interested in having my own website. This Internet is amazing!"

Sharon rolled her eyes. "He's hooked on the damn thing. Every night he and Brad have a fight over whose turn it is to use the computer. Bill was up till 2 O'clock this morning surfing the net. Look at his eyes; don't they look like little computer terminals to you?" They'd all laughed.

Joking with Arnie and Jane, Bill had felt quite optimistic. There was this world of opportunity out there, just waiting to be explored. He would find what he was searching for. He just had to keep positive.

That night he experienced his first panic attack. It had started when he'd casually looked at his bank statement. His eyes skimmed through all the transactions and stopped at the bottom line: - $14,000. He looked at this figure in dismay. How could they have an overdraft of this amount? He couldn't breathe. $14,000! He had never been able to save that amount when he was working. How would they ever pay it back now that he was unemployed? He sank his head in his hands. His neck and shoulder muscles started throbbing. The ache spread to his arms and stomach. He needed to find a job. No, not just a job – a high paying job. And he needed to find it soon. In the meantime, he and his family had to cut down on their spending.

He and Sharon had argued that night. He'd put together a list of things they could do to save money. There were 25 items on the list. For example, they could stop entertaining so much. This would save them $100 a month. Then there was shopping. Did they really need to spend so much on convenience foods, when fresh food cost so much less? They were spending quite a bit on electricity. Did Sharon know how often she boiled a full kettle when all she needed was a single cup of coffee? Sharon listened, her irritation mounting with every cost-saving idea. Then she launched her counterattack. "How much do you spend every time you 'network' over lunch with one of your contacts? Do you know how many kettles I could boil with that amount? As for convenience foods, if you want to save the money, you do the shopping, and you can prepare our meals." Bill was silent. He couldn't understand why they were arguing about kettles when he was being sucked into a vortex of dread. He lay awake listening to Sharon tossing and turning. He had to find a way out of this nightmare. He had to get back to where he'd been before, well before Chuck had destroyed his life.

The interview with Christine at the Sportsman's Warehouse went well. Bill seemed to fit all the requirements for the position of merchandising manager. The only issue they needed to discuss further was how he'd feel about reporting to a 25 year old. He hoped he sounded convincing when he said it would be "No problem."

His second interview was a disappointment. He didn't like Macy's. Although the job itself was better than the Sportsman's Warehouse one – he'd be managing a store – it felt stuffy and boring. Everyone seemed to walk around with plastic smiles upon their faces. He wondered if he would be able to inject some real warmth into the culture.

He went home feeling quite dejected. Later that day he got calls from both Sportsman's Warehouse and Macy's, both of whom wanted him to come for a second interview. He tried to get hold of Sharon at work to tell her the good news, but she was unavailable. Brad was still at school. He looked around. There was nothing to do. He decided to go out for a walk.

He caught a bus to the old part of town. He loved the architecture of the old buildings and the feeling of being transported into another age, another world. He breathed in the aroma of freshly baked bread and watched the deli assistant ladle chicken soup into plastic tubs. Just past the coffee shop, where he'd spent half an hour sipping freshly ground coffee, he discovered an old bookshop. As he entered the shop, he felt as though he was walking into a Dickens novel. A wizened old man, dressed in a grey suit, shuffled around, carefully returning books to their rightful places. He noticed the oregan pine bookcases which housed the treasures. How he loved old wood, he thought, running his hand along the grain. His eyes were drawn to a green, leather bound book on the top shelf. He stretched up to take the book. It fell out of his grasp raising a cloud of dust, as it hit the ground. Something fell out of the book. He bent over to pick it up and recognised the tiger instantly. He flipped over the card eagerly anticipating its wisdom, and read:

You deserve more

He looked around guiltily. The owner was busy in the back room. He slipped the card into the book and casually walked to the counter to wait for the Dickens character to return. The bookstore owner commented on his choice of book, and Bill mumbled a response. He didn't even know the title of the book he'd just purchased.

He felt strangely uplifted. These cards seemed to appear every time he needed them. He didn't understand how, or even why. Why had he come to this part of town today? What had drawn him into the bookstore? And why had he chosen that very book? He didn't know. It was as though he was meant to discover this card today. He looked at the message again.

You deserve more.

That was obvious. It felt right. He did deserve more. But he couldn't quite define what 'more' meant to him. He felt strangely dissatisfied with the direction he was going in. But he couldn't explain it to anyone else. It was obvious that he needed a high paying job. He knew his experience made him suitable to the retail and particularly the clothing industry. But the jobs he was interviewing for left him feeling strangely dissatisfied. They paid well, but something was missing. Something he couldn't quite define.

Sharon wasn't home. Where was she? It wasn't like her to be so late. He had so much to tell her about the day's coincidences. He felt so good. He did deserve more after all. He just needed to clarify what was missing in his life. He suddenly recalled how Di had recommended this woman, Rose, to him. Rose was a business strategist who counselled CEOs on their careers. Di's boss had been helped by her, when she'd been retrenched. "What the hell," he thought. "I'm in a crazy mood today already." He booked an appointment.

The next day he found himself driving through the wooded area of Marietta. As he drove through the gates he was struck by the beauty of her home. The small white cottage, with its wooden sash windows and a grey slate roof, nestled in a garden awash with colour. Rows of red, pink and white azaleas lined the cobbled path. And there at the front door stood a short dark woman dressed in a navy and teal polka dot suit.

"Welcome to Tranquility," she smiled as she led him to

a cast iron chair in the garden. It was under the cherry tree, sipping lime and soda, that he found himself telling her everything. His battle with Papas, the jobs he was interviewing for and how he still felt that something was missing. She listened intently, nodding at intervals. He immediately felt she understood what he was going through. She asked him how he was feeling about it all.

"I don't really know," he responded.

"Maybe a little confused, and even a bit vulnerable?" she offered. He looked surprised. She was spot on.

"And you were probably feeling very frustrated and out of control a little earlier?"

He was amazed at her insight. How did you know all this?" he asked. "Are you reading my mind?"

"No, I'm not psychic," she laughed. "You're experiencing a major change in your life right now. I'm simply describing the emotions most people feel when they go through different phases of transformation. "You see," she explained, "There is a cycle of change we all share". She began drawing two circles, one at the top of the page, and the other at the bottom. She labelled the first circle 'control' and the second one 'chaos'. "In change," she explained, "we move between the two emotional states of 'control' and 'chaos' over and over again. Let me explain how. Before any major change, we usually feel 'in control'. Nothing really changes until something or somebody pushes us out of our comfort zone. For you it was being fired. For others it may be a divorce, or moving cities. Whatever the change is, our first natural response is to resist it. We don't enjoy being 'out of our comfort zones'. We want to feel 'normal', confident and in control again. As we resist the inevitable shove into chaos, we experience feelings of anger, frustration, and even bitterness. Life seems very unfair.

Bill thought of his war against Papas, and nodded.

"At some stage we realise we can't get back what we've lost. We release our hold on the past..."

Bill remembered the day he decided to stop fighting Papas.

" ...and when that happens, we are hurled into chaos. Chaos is a time when we feel extremely vulnerable. We are lost. We feel scared. Nothing seems to work for us anymore. Everything is so confusing. We no longer want the old way, but we're unsure of what we do want."

"That is exactly how I'm feeling," he observed. "What happens next?"

"Well," she pointed to her diagram, "we know that when we inject chaos into order, the result is resistance. Forming order out of chaos, on the other hand, is the way to creativity." Noticing Bill's bewilderment she explained further. "Chaos is the perfect time to discover meaning. When nothing around us makes sense any longer, we tend to look inwards. We try to discover who we were, who we are and who we could be. We begin to experiment with new ideas, new thoughts and new values. Suddenly we discover within ourselves an intuition that we didn't know we had. An inner voice which has been stifled by structure, routine and responsibility, suddenly demands to be heard. We find ourselves becoming increasingly spontaneous. We are drawn to places we haven't visited for years. We begin to experience coincidences and synchronicity."

"That's it!" exclaimed Bill. "That has definitely been happening to me lately." He carefully took out the tiger cards and explained how he'd discovered them.

Rose tried to interpret the mystery: "You've been experiencing a lot of coincidences lately. These cards seem to be the key to this synchronicity. They contain important messages that seem to come to you when you need them. Where they are leading you to, I cannot say. It is something only you can discover. But it seems to me like you've been chosen for something very special."

He suddenly felt grounded. There was a reason for all of this. He had a special purpose. He just had to discover what it was.

She looked at her watch. "My next appointment is arriving in 15 minutes. If you'd like, I could give you some exercises to do, that will help you to clarify things for yourself." She handed him two sealed envelopes with the words "values" printed on each.

"These activities will help you to discover your own unique set of values. Values are beliefs or principles we have about what is important in our lives. Each of us has our own unique blueprint of values which is shaped by our culture, background and our experiences. Our inner meaning is often tied up in our values. By uncovering our values, we can discover our special purpose. Once you know your special purpose, you will understand the feelings that are flowing through you. Then you'll know what to do."

A feeling of excitement shot through Bill. He was keen to begin the exercises at once.

"These are very powerful exercises," Rose warned. "They are powerful because they help you to draw out your subconscious thoughts and desires. But remember your inner self is a shy creature. It will only emerge when you are alone, feeling relaxed and are unlikely to be interrupted. Also know that you'll be working at quite deep levels of your psyche. If at any time you feel uncomfortable, or concerned, please come and see me."

Bill rushed home, dying to try out the exercises. There was a note from Sharon saying Brad would be eating dinner at a friend's house, and she wouldn't be home until after 8 O'clock. He should eat without them. "Synchronicity strikes again," he thought, amused. This was an ideal time to do his inner work.

He picked up the first envelope and read through the instructions:

1) Find a quiet space.
2) Take a few clean sheets of paper and a pencil.
3) Jot down the first things that come into your mind.
4) Draw two axes of a graph on your page. The 'y' (longitudinal) axis represents how you have felt about events in your life. -10 represents feelings of anger, boredom, depression, low self-esteem, or frustration. 0 represents feeling neutral. +10 represents

feelings of excitement, motivation, pride, self confidence and contentment. The 'x' (horizontal) axis represents the years of your life in five year periods.

5) Now draw a graph of your life showing times you felt extremely positive or negative about yourself. Try to remember specific incidents e.g. the day you married, the day you left your first job. Label each incident and jot down key words that describe why you felt positive or negative about the event.

6) When you have completed your graph, look inside envelope 2 for instructions on how to interpret what you've done.

Bill drew the axes of his graph. He tried to fill in the specific incidents from the beginning of his life. His memories were cloudy. He looked at the end of the graph. There was one incident that was crystal clear. The day he'd been fired. He recalled Roger's words "Sorry Bill, but you'll have to go..." Suddenly the feelings of disbelief, shock and anger surged through his pen. He looked down. The flood of frustration from the last six months took up one small section on his graph. He noticed that everything he'd written reflected his time at Papas. He needed to write about his life before Papas. He sat, with his pen poised, thinking. There was nothing there. He tried harder to remember. It was more difficult than he'd expected. He found himself peering through a fog of frustrations, disappointments, and responsibility as he tried to connect with the Bill of his youth. He closed his eyes and waited. An image began to form. He looked inwards. There was 16 year old Bill, standing triumphant holding a racquet above his head. He'd finally beaten Phil at racquet ball. He was replaced by a fit 20 year old who went jogging everyday with his sister and her friend. He fell into a trance. His pen seemed to lift in his hand and he began writing urgently. Image after image flooded his consciousness. He saw Pat and Sharon cheering him on as he won his first 10km race. His parents beaming as he graduated. A young Bill was reading poetry as he proposed to the softly spoken Sharon. A dreamer, telling Sharon of his plans to change the world. As the memories became clearer, the feelings associated with those times pulsated in his veins. Pride, joy, hope, a sense of freedom, self confidence, excitement, and positive energy. He began to smile. He'd had some good times in his life. And now, it was almost as though he'd forgotten how to enjoy himself. What had stopped him doing all these things he loved so much, he wondered.

The mysterious force left his body. He felt drained. He got up. He put on the kettle. He looked at his watch. 8 O'clock. What had happened to the time? He heard the key in the latch. Sharon and Brad were greeting him. Sharon was asking him what he'd had for supper. Supper? He'd forgotten to eat. It was strange, but he didn't feel hungry. Brad was hyped up about the latest website he'd discovered. Sharon was looking radiant. She'd had a great day at work. Bill felt subdued. He tried to describe his day, but it seemed so irrelevant when he put it into words. Yesterday he'd gone to a bookstore and found a card. Today he met a counsellor and did some thinking about his life. So what! He remembered Rose's warning. "Be careful who you try to share your discoveries with. The power of inner work can only be understood by those who have experienced it for themselves."

The next day he began his new life. From his graph he drew up a list of what had made him feel positive about life. He looked at his list. It was all so obvious. He needed to jog, play racquet ball, lose weight, spend more time with the people he cared for, get music, nature, and poetry back into his life. He needed a job that not only paid well, but that had meaning. He was amazed. After only one exercise he had the clarity he needed. Rose was right. This inner work was powerful. He phoned Rose to thank her. She congratulated him. "You've got your life's strategic plan together, now all you have to do is live it. It's like implementing a strategy. Easy to say, harder to do."

He knew he could live out the life he wanted. All he had to do was to set some targets and action plans. He'd play racquet ball twice a week, jog three times a week, take his family out to dinner once a week, cut beer out of his diet, and read a book once a week.

Full of determination, he picked up the phone. It was time to start on his first action step. He was going to ask Phil for a game of racquet ball. Phil was surprised to get a call from Bill. "Funny you should phone, but Harry has just cancelled and I have a court for this evening at 6 O'clock." Bill accepted. "I'd better warn you that I'm unfit."

"No excuses and no mercy," laughed Phil.

The first game had been awful. Bill hadn't realised just how unfit he'd become. Not wanting to admit how much his legs were hurting, Bill had continued playing till the lights went out. Phil got the drinks as Bill flopped gratefully against the wall. He felt exhausted. His muscles ached. But he felt invigorated. He was back. He'd missed his racquet ball, and his friendships. He found that even after all this time apart, Phil and he could still chat easily. Phil now owned his own strategic planning consultancy.

"Sometimes being fired is the best thing that could happen to you," Phil had said thoughtfully. "I should know – that's how I started my own business, and I haven't looked back since."

On hearing that Bill was looking for a job in the retail clothing industry, Phil became quite excited. "What a coincidence. I've just finished doing some consulting for a company called Branded Apparel who manufacture and sell branded clothing in the US. They have a few factories in developing countries that haven't been performing and they're looking to fix that. I've just helped them to develop a new strategy for globalising their business and I know they're looking for people with your experience. If you want to give me your resume, I'll pass it on to them."

It was strange how many coincidences he had experienced since he had become open to them. That week Bill found himself bumping into a number of his old business school colleagues. At the bookstore he chanced upon Pauline, who'd dropped out of the corporate world to start her own dress designing business. She recalled how she'd got into her own business. She'd made the decision after 'writing her own obituary.' Bill looked puzzled. "It's a powerful technique for discovering your life's mission." She explained. "You imagine yourself at your own funeral sometime in the distant future. Then you have to write what you'd like to hear people say about you and the way you lived your life. I did this exercise three years ago, and it gave me quite a fright. I discovered there was a lot I needed to change in my life. At that time I weighed six kilograms more than I do today. My cholesterol and blood pressure were dangerously high, and I was continually suffering from stress. I never had time for myself or for my friends. My doctor actually told me if I didn't look after myself, I was going to have a heart attack. Today I'm healthy, happy and enjoying myself. I'd never go back."

She listened to Bill's story with sympathy. When he told her he was interviewing with Branded Apparel, she'd become quite animated. "They are my biggest and best client," she'd enthused. She promised to put in a good word about him.

While jogging in the park, he'd stumbled across another business school contact. Karen gave him her business card. Caron Oldstein. Self development facilitator.

"Didn't you used to be Karen?" he asked. Caron, who'd always seemed a little odd, explained how an 'O,' being a circle, represented completion and inner harmony. After doing journal therapy, which involved keeping a daily journal of her life, she'd created a new path for herself. Her name, as it was spelled now, reflected her new-found tranquillity. She gave him a number of 'alternative techniques' he could use to 'get in touch with himself.'

'Bill thought back to the 14 weeks since he'd settled with Papas. He'd met so many people. He'd learned so much about himself. He'd done things he'd never thought possible. As well as going on nine job interviews, he had tried reflexology and yoga. He'd seen a metaphysician, who'd helped him channel his energy positively. He sat for hours absorbed in classical music. He'd consumed books on Tao, Zen, Buddhism and New Age thinking. The other night he had sat on his roof and watched the sun set. The neighbours thought he'd gone mad, but it had been an awesome experience. Now he understood what that card about the sunset had meant. The message in *You deserve more* had finally been revealed to him. Like a trickle charger, he had found a way to tap into the power of the universe.

The only person who understood what he was experiencing was Rose. Sharon wasn't impressed by the power of the universe. She was more interested in paying the bills on time. Pat was concerned about what her brother was getting involved in. "I hope you're not talking about this esoteric stuff during your interviews," she remarked.

He wasn't that stupid. He knew most people were threatened by anything that smacked of the mysterious. He used to be that way himself. But now he felt comforted by the coincidences he'd experienced lately. It was all happening for a reason. He did have a special purpose.

And it was tied somehow to Branded Apparel. He knew he was going to work for them.

The interview with Branded Apparel had been a mere formality. From the start he'd been quite excited about their dream of creating centres of excellence all over the world. His job, the HR director explained, would be to develop a strategy for putting this concept into practice. For his research he would need to familiarise himself with every aspect of the company's operations including marketing, branding, manufacturing, and distribution. He would then visit all their factories trying to discover pockets of excellence. Then he'd put together a strategy for replicating these pockets of excellence globally. "And from there, you can create your own job. The possibilities are endless."

He'd accepted immediately, and found himself hurled into a whirlwind of activity. On the plane home from San Francisco three months later, he found himself describing the adrenalin rush his job gave him, to the passenger beside him. "In the last three months I've caught 30 planes, visited 54 sites, and have met 300 new people. I've put together a major strategy which was immediately accepted by my company. And today I've just received a fax from my boss telling me how much they appreciate the work I've done and they've given me an increase. My wife will be ecstatic." Life had never been better.

He arrived home. The house was in darkness again. Where was Sharon? She was never at home lately. He wanted to celebrate his increase with her. As he climbed the stairs to the front door, he suddenly had a strange sense of foreboding. Something wasn't right. He put the key into the lock, and turned on the lights. The house felt empty. He rushed to their room. Sharon's clothes were missing. He tore into Brad's room. It was neat. Too neat. The computer was gone. The sense of panic rose in his throat as he dashed from room to room, flinging open cupboards. He found the note on the kitchen table. It was all over. Sharon and Brad had left him.

4 The Search for the Elusive Tiger

Life is either a daring adventure or nothing

— Helen Keller

He tracked them down to an apartment in Manhattan. Sharon wasn't pleased to see him.

"It's over Bill," she said. "I'm sorry."

"But why?" he demanded. "With me getting this job, I thought everything had finally come right for us!"

"For you, Bill. Things came right for you. You got the job you wanted. I'm sorry, but I can't continue standing on the fringes of your life watching you chase one obsession after another. I deserve more than that."

The dull pain that had been seeping through his body when he found her note oozed into his heart. He tried to understand. What more did she expect from him? He'd been trying so hard for so long. Why did she have to do this just as things were finally turning around? He couldn't believe it. There had to be something else. Something he should have seen a long time ago, but didn't. Something that would explain her constant disappearances from home. His eyes suddenly focused on the tennis racquet in the hall. No one in his family played tennis. Like a worn out punching bag, he waited for the next blow. "Have you found someone else?" he demanded.

"Yes," she responded.

The blanket of grief descended, smothering him. He had to get out of the apartment immediately. He needed to be alone. He staggered down the stairs, drunk with despair. He didn't want to know anymore. He didn't want to imagine them together. He just had to get away.

In his hotel room, the flood gates opened. A torrent of emotions – anger, betrayal, and misery, surged out. He couldn't understand what was happening to him. Why was his life so impossibly difficult? All he was trying to do was to make everyone happy. He'd worked so hard, but it wasn't good enough. All the people he cared about most had betrayed him. First Roger, then Peter, and now Sharon. Why had she done this to him? He didn't deserve this.

The deluge subsided. He felt drained of all energy. He stared at the blank television set wondering when it would ever stop. He'd been fighting the rapids for so long, he couldn't face any more white water. A thought bubbled up. He knew what he'd do. He'd win her back. A wave of exhaustion swamped the idea.

"Life is strange," mused Sharon a month later. For six years she'd tried to get Bill's attention, but work had always come first. She had constantly asked him to spend more time with her and Brad, but he had never listened. She'd supported him when he'd been fired, hoping that the experience would change him. But it never did. He'd simply focused his energy on all that esoteric stuff. Then, when he'd got his job at Branded Apparel, he'd once again ignored her and Brad, as he flitted from city to city. It was just like Papas all over again. He was an incurable workaholic. He was never going to change. Then she'd left him. All of a sudden he was able to take time off his precious work to win her back. He kept appearing at her door behind a bunch of flowers. At first she'd felt vindicated by his attempts to pursue her. Then she'd felt a tinge of pity as he pleaded with her, promising to change. Promising to be everything she wanted him to be. But she knew Bill too well. He was only really happy when he was striving to achieve some impossible challenge. And that left little space for anything else in his life. Later she felt irritated by his constant visits, phone calls and messages. He wouldn't accept no for an answer, and he was becoming a source of conflict in her new relationship with Tony. She needed to get on with her life, and he was preventing that from happening. She didn't want to hurt him, but she had to do something to get him to understand. And so, the words that would torment him for months were spoken.

"Bill, the one lesson you seem to have trouble learning in life, is when to let go. It destroyed you at Papas. It is going to destroy you again if you don't listen now. Our marriage is over. Nothing you can do will ever bring it back. You have to let go. For my sake, Brad's sake and your own, go away, and try to build a new life for yourself." He'd been wounded by her words, but at least he'd finally got the message. He'd left.

Back in Atlanta Bill tried to get on with his life. But it all seemed so pointless. His passion for work had dissolved. He had no energy for racquet ball. He stopped bothering to socialise with Pat, Peter, Jane and Arnie. They had become so careful in the way they treated him, that he felt uncomfortable being with them. He tried to resume his 'inner work', but that proved to be simply boring. He saw Caron as he drifted through a bookstore, looking for inspiration. She was going on about 'auras' or something. He decided she was definitely a crackpot. One he could do without.

The only person who understood how he was feeling was Rose. He would spend hours in her garden just talking about 'where he was at'. She simply listened, and sympathised. Once she made an attempt at humour.

"It sounds like you've just entered another change cycle," she observed. "Do you enjoy all this resistance and chaos or are you simply a masochist?"

"Definitely a masochist," he agreed. It was the first time he'd laughed in a long time.

She became serious. "Remember how awful you felt after Papas had fired you?"

He nodded.

"And do you remember how suddenly, when you were ready for it, you began to experience synchronicity? Remember how the tiger cards kept finding you when you needed a special message? And do you remember how you began playing racquet ball with Phil, and how he in turn led you to Branded Apparel? And how you felt your destiny was somehow tied up with this company?"

Bill nodded again.

"I still believe you have a special purpose in life, and that these things are happening to you for a reason. Maybe you need to be free of your past, in order to fulfil your destiny."

"I'm not sure I have the energy for it," laughed Bill. But he felt comforted by her words.

A few days later, Bill's boss had called him into his office.

"How would you like a real challenge, Bill?

"Sure!" Bill's interest was peaked.

"It's all happening in South Africa."

"What is?" asked Bill.

"We have a small factory in Johannesburg that is just not producing results. It is currently being managed by a local, a Jannie Engelbrecht, whom we have our doubts about. We believe the factory has a lot of potential. The South African currency has just devalued, making labour there very cheap. South Africa could become one of our manufacturing nodes for our globalisation strategy. We want to put in some real leadership, and give it a go for a year. If it doesn't work out, we'll close our operations down and relocate the factory to Malaysia. We want you to go and shake up the place a bit. We believe you have what it takes to do the job for us."

Exactly a month later, as Bill boarded his flight to

South Africa, he felt a surge of adrenalin energise his entire being. He couldn't believe he was actually doing it. He was off to Africa. Everyone had cautioned him against going to such a dangerous place. Their warnings had sounded quite ominous.

"Africa is in the midst of an Aids epidemic. What do you want to risk yourself for?"

"Johannesburg is the most dangerous city in the world. The criminals run the show. Government has no control whatsoever."

"Armed robbers break into homes and torture their victims before stealing whatever they want."

"The hijackers there don't just steal your car – they shoot you in the head first."

"It's the Wild West out there. You have to be crazy to even consider going," they warned.

Bill smiled. Yes he did feel a touch crazy. The feeling exhilarated him. He remembered how at first he'd been reluctant to take up the challenge. But Rose had helped him see it differently.

"A journey is often used as a metaphor for life," she'd mused. "In mythology, the hero always undergoes an odyssey, as part of his mission. Maybe your special purpose is waiting for you in Africa." He'd felt a stirring of expectation at her words, but remained unconvinced.

"What is holding you back?" she'd asked. He thought of his life without Sharon and Brad. "Nothing," he admitted.

"Well maybe," she said gently, "maybe it's time to let

go". She stood up and walked to her bookcase. " I have a gift for you," she said, as she reached for a book. I found this poem that reminded me of your cards, and I thought you'd like to take it with you. It goes like this:

Life is like a wild tiger.
You can either lie down
and let it lay its paw upon your head
Or sit on its back and ride it.
Ride the wild tiger.

"This could be your wild tiger," she whispered. "The greatest adventure of your life. A trip to South Africa. Or the Rainbow Nation as it is called. Who knows, at the end of the rainbow, you might just find your pot of gold."

Bill fastened his seat belt. As the aeroplane lifted off the ground, Bill thought of the symbolism. There was no turning back.

"Excuse me, can I borrow your magazine?" Bill looked at the stout black man sitting in the window seat next to him. His chubby hands were covered in thick gold rings. Dressed in a sweat shirt and jeans, the amiable man beside him could have been anyone.

"Sure," replied Bill. "Where are you from?"

Jerry Khumalo, the businessman from Soweto formally introduced himself to Bill. When he heard Bill was visiting South Africa for the first time, he began speaking passionately about his country. He described the dynamic pulse of Johannesburg, the City of Gold. The place where ordinary people could become millionaires. His enthusiasm was infectious.

Jerry listened intently as Bill described his plans for turning around the Branded Apparel factory in Johannesburg.

"In South Africa we'd call that 'transformation'. You know I'm also involved in transforming the transportation industry in our country."

"I don't understand." Bill was confused.

Jerry quickly changed the subject. "What you are doing is a good thing for our people," he declared. "It will create more jobs for us. We must help you to succeed in whatever way we can." He dabbed away the sweat forming on his brow, and took another sip of his brandy and coke.

"What do you understand about our culture?" he asked.

"Nothing."

"You are going to need to know black culture to succeed. I can talk to you about it, if you like."

"Thank you, I'd appreciate that," responded Bill gratefully.

"I just need to go," he pointed to the toilet "and then we can talk."

As Jerry pushed past him, Bill noticed something fall from his pocket. He leant down to pick up the all too familiar card. Its message made him smile:

let go and the world will come to you

"Excuse me, but you dropped this."

Jerry grabbed the card without as much as a thank-you and shuffled off.

Bill eagerly awaited Jerry's return. He couldn't believe how at the start of the journey, he found someone who also knew about the cards. Maybe the mystery of the tiger would be revealed to him, at last.

On returning to his seat, Jerry appeared distant. Bill tried to resume their discussion, but Jerry replied in a way that clearly discouraged further conversation. Bill couldn't understand what had caused this change of heart. When Bill tried to discuss the tiger card, Jerry denied having seen any such card.

"Before you went to the toilet, I picked up a card you'd dropped. It had the words *let go and the world will come to you* printed on it," Bill insisted.

"Where is the card now?" demanded Jerry.

"I gave it back to you. But I want you to tell me what it all means."

Jerry's response caused Bill to shudder.

"Don't get involved in things you know nothing about," he warned. "It could become very dangerous. Africa is not like America."

"But I do know about these cards," insisted Bill. "I discovered them for myself in the United States."

The sinister shadow faded, and the genial Jerry returned, oozing charm out of every pore.

"What cards did you find, and where did you find them?" he enquired.

Bill explained how he'd found the first card about the sunset in his in-tray. How the second card he'd tripped over in the street, and how the third card had been hidden in an old book. He explained how each card had suddenly appeared at a critical point in his life. He remarked how only recently he'd had to learn the lesson of 'letting go' and how Jerry's card was particularly relevant to him now. Jerry was intrigued. He asked to see the cards, but Bill had unfortunately left them in his luggage. Jerry then excused himself and fell promptly asleep.

As the plane began its descent into Johannesburg International Airport, a wave of apprehension rolled through Bill. He took a deep breath. "Time to ride the tiger," he vowed.

Before the seat belt lights had been switched off, Jerry had collected his belongings. As the doors opened he strode off the plane into a waiting Mercedes Benz. The car had disappeared by the time the rest of the passengers began to disembark.

The queues at immigration were moving quite quickly. Within 10 minutes he should be collecting his luggage, hopping on a magic mini-bus which would take him to his hotel. He wondered where he'd find the bus. Within minutes he was at the head of the line. The bureaucrat at immigration looked quite bored. He inspected Bill's papers and stared at Bill.

"Is this your passport?" he demanded.

"Yes," replied Bill.

The official paged through the passport again.

"Is there any problem?" asked Bill. The immigration official ignored him, examined the computer screen, and then checked Bill's passport again.

"Stay here," he ordered. He left the booth taking Bill's passport with him. Bill waited impatiently. All the other passengers were moving rapidly through immigration. Fifteen minutes later, everyone from his plane had left the hall. He was standing alone. He began to panic. "Where had the man gone with his passport? Why was he taking so long? A new planeload of passengers had begun to go through. Bill suddenly saw the immigration officer at the end of the hall chatting to someone. Bill felt angry. But there was nothing he could do. He had to wait. Finally the immigration official returned. He stamped Bill's passport and waved him through, without so much as an apology.

Bill collected a trolley at the baggage section and looked for the carousel for his flight. American Airlines flight 302 from New York was not listed. Bill looked around. Most of his fellow passengers had already cleared customs. He began to feel anxious. He suddenly saw a woman who'd been on his flight, coming out of the toilets, pushing a trolley laden with luggage.

He raced to her. "Where did you find your baggage?" he asked. She pointed to a carousel. "From that round-about – but it stopped about 10 minutes ago. I didn't see any luggage left on it. Why don't you try the lost baggage section," she offered.

Cheryl at the South African Airway's lost baggage counter was most helpful and apologetic. After a few phone calls, she managed to track down Bill's luggage to Durban. For some strange reason, his baggage had gone onto a connecting flight. She took down his contact details and promised to have his luggage delivered to his hotel within six hours.

There were four other passengers on the bus: a business women who lived in Sandton, a German youth, and an old English couple. They soon began chatting amongst themselves. When they heard that Bill had lost his luggage, they sympathised: "It happens all the time," remarked the English man. They began comparing stories of lost baggage. But when Bill told them how he'd been harassed at immigration, the Sandton business woman looked puzzled.

"That sounds very strange. I've never heard of immigration hassling anyone before. I wonder what they were looking for?" Bill looked out of the back window. He kept seeing the same grey BMW behind them. He suspected they were being followed. As they turned into the driveway of his hotel, he noticed the car pass by. He felt distinctly uneasy.

The hotel receptionist was friendly and efficient. "We're sorry about your introduction to South Africa. We'll try to make the rest of your stay much more pleasant. As soon as your bags arrive, we'll have them sent up to your room."

The room was standard Holiday Inn. Bill switched on the TV set. He looked at the drama taking place on the screen. A security van carrying two million dollars had been ambushed on a highway outside Johannesburg. Three guards were lying dead on the ground. A fourteen year old girl had been gang raped and left to die. The community had burnt down the homes of the suspected rapists. A pipe bomb had exploded in Cape Town city centre, outside the police station. This was the news at 8 O'clock. He picked up the newspapers. The words 'fraud', 'crime', 'break-in', 'hijacking' and 'murder' caught his eye, time and time again. He couldn't believe he'd left the safety of the United States for this.

He went to the hotel restaurant for dinner. When he returned, his bags were already in his room. He ran a bath and began to unpack. Everything was there, as he'd packed it. He breathed a sigh of relief. He'd been over-reacting. It had all just been a terrible mistake. There was nothing to worry about after all. He suddenly thought of the cards. Where were they? He'd forgotten where he'd packed them. He began searching through his cases. He found the card of the sunset, and the one about fairness. But he couldn't find the card *You Deserve More*. He wondered what he'd done with it.

On Friday morning he awoke from a disturbed sleep. In his dream he'd been desperately searching for a tiger card. He knew that if he could just escape from Jerry and his bodyguards and get to the light, he'd find the card he was looking for. Just as Jerry and his dogs were closing in on him his alarm clock buzzed him awake. He opened his eyes, looked at the strange surroundings, and tried to make some sense of where he was. He remembered

Rose's voice. "Perhaps this is your wild tiger, your mission." He smiled. He was ready to begin his quest.

At breakfast, sipping his coffee, he began to plan his day. It was Friday and he had until Monday to 'settle in' before starting work officially. His aim today was to hire a car, buy a map of the city and visit the Branded Apparel factory. The hotel receptionist proved most helpful. She booked an Avis car for 10 O'clock. Meanwhile he could find a map of the city in Exclusive Books, which was in the shopping mall attached to the hotel.

Sandton City Mall was enormous. Under its upmarket glass dome, it housed all the usual boutiques and supermarkets, as well as a range of specialist stores selling everything from computers to art equipment. He suddenly imagined Sharon and Jane in this shopping centre. How they would have loved the variety. He immediately brushed the thought away. He found a bookstore and bought a map of the city. At their coffee bar he ordered a cappuccino, and looked up Umkhonto House, Number 20 Beacon Road, Doornfontein on the map. It was quite far from his hotel. He might need to find accommodation closer to the factory.

At 10 O'clock he was on his way. He took the M1 South to 'town', and then headed west to Beacon Road. He found number 20 easily enough. He parked up the street and picked his way through the litter, to his new workplace. He noticed the prostitutes lining the streets, the holes in the pavements and the general neglect of the buildings. A faint smell of urine filled the air. A few teenagers loitering around Umkhonto House directed him to the second floor. As he walked up the stairs he noticed a layer of dust on the railings. He breathed in the musty air and made a mental note to sort out the maintenance of the building. At the top of the stairs he gazed at the large, single room which constituted the Branded Apparel factory. The place looked a mess. Clothes, in various stages of completion were draped over chairs, spilling out of boxes, or dumped in piles on a floor that obviously never got swept. Sullen workers went about their tasks with little enthusiasm. As he walked past them, the employees stared at him suspiciously.

"Ah, you must be the new boss." A thin, pale man, with greased back brown hair and black rimmed glasses came forward, his hand outstretched. Wearing crimpolene fawn trousers and a light blue shirt, he looked like a relic from the 1950's.

"We were only expecting you to arrive on Monday. I'm Jannie Engelbrecht, the factory manager."

Bill held out his hand. "I'm Bill. Pleased to meet you."

He noticed the workers staring at him. Before he could introduce himself to them, Jannie was leading him into a small office. As he was shuttting the door he shouted at a large black lady in pink overalls.

"Doris, we'd like some coffee."

"Yes mmm," mumbled Doris.

Jannie began welcoming Bill to South Africa. "It's good to have an expert from the US here to show us the way," remarked Jannie. "In South Africa, most companies are behind the times. But I've been very interested in world class practices. During the last two years I have designed a Quality Management system for Branded Apparel. It is a privilege to have someone like you here at last who can appreciate it all..."

Bill felt the revulsion well up in his throat. "Not again," he thought. "Not over my dead body!"

Before he could say anything, Jannie had pulled out eight ring binder files and began to show off the work he'd done on developing a Quality Management system for Branded Apparel. Bill tried to explain that he didn't believe in Quality Management, but Jannie was not about to be interrupted. He showed off page after page, manual after manual to an unwilling hostage.

Bill finally got his attention. "I only have an hour here, and I'd like to see round the factory and meet the staff."

"Of course," replied Jannie, in a tone of disappointment, "I'll give you a tour."

Jannie took on the role of benevolent father, and escorted Bill around the factory, introducing him to all the workers. Their reaction was less than welcoming. "This is Doris, our teagirl," he said pointing to the lady who'd brought their coffee. Doris stared at the floor and mumbled a greeting. "And Jay our buyer." A thin Indian man looked at him and Jannie with contempt. "This is Rosalie from marketing." An attractive woman with a golden skin shyly nodded a greeting. Quiet stocky Koos, simply shook Bill's hand whilst Nandi, a striking black woman with braids in her hair stared at him sceptically.

Bill wondered how he was going to break down the wall of distrust that appeared between him and the group. Then he noticed a tall muscular black man who seemed to radiate energy.

"And this," announced Jannie "is Vuse, our local *kaffirtjie*". Vuse laughed without any humour and responded something along the lines of 'witman'. Bill could sense the antagonism between them. The introductions left Bill feeling uncomfortable. He hadn't expected to be welcomed by a wall of suspicion, distrust and contempt. "How am I ever going to build a team of excellence from this lot?" he wondered.

Jannie steered him into his office. "Coming from America, you're going to find these people different," he stated. "You have to understand their culture in order to work with them." Once Jannie began talking, nothing could stop him. "The blacks here are lazy. They don't like to work. So if you don't watch them all the time, they won't do anything. You have to know how to talk to them if you want to get anything done. I grew up on a farm with them so I know them well. If you want to communicate with them, just ask me. I'll be happy to help."

"Tell me about Vuse," asked Bill. "He seems to have something special about him."

Jannie's face flushed in anger. "Don't let him fool you. Vuse is a born troublemaker. He stirs up discontent amongst the workers all the time. Before he joined us we never had a strike. Now he's always causing trouble with the workers. He thinks because he's black he can do anything he wants and the government will protect him." A torrent of frustration flooded out of Jannie's mouth as he began to explain how difficult it had been for him as a white manager in the new South Africa. "They've brought in this new labour legislation, which means you can't fire anyone anymore. They can sit around all day and there is nothing you can do to them. Unless you catch them in the act of stealing, or burning the factory down, you can't fire them. So they just do what they like." He then started complaining about some new legislation called Employment Equity. "You can't just hire anyone you like here. They have to be black or coloured. I'm not a racist, but to me that is just reverse discrimination. There is no place for the white male anymore in the new South Africa." For the next 10 minutes Jannie spat out hatred and bitterness about the new South Africa. Bill felt himself being consumed by negativity, hopelessness, frustration and anger.

Bill finally stood up firmly. "I must go now. I'll see you on Monday at 8 O'clock," he heard himself saying. As he walked across the factory, the workers stopped sewing and watched him leave. As he scurried down the stairs he heard a cheeky "Goodbye Mr America" breaking the silence. Then some tittering. The memory of Vuse's chuckle stayed with him until he reached the car.

As he took the M1 North back to Sandton, he felt relieved to be out of Jannie's clutches, away from the sullen workers, out of the dusty, grimy building and back into civilisation. He wondered how he was ever going to manage to motivate himself to go back on Monday. When Bob had mentioned the word 'challenge', he obviously didn't know how bad the situation was. He worried how he was going to handle working with Jannie and Vuse.

On returning to the hotel, he felt the need to shower away the revulsion he felt. As he dressed he felt a little better. He decided to visit Exclusive Books for a cappuccino and a bit of inspiration. He found the esoteric section easily. They had a great selection. He spotted a number of books Rose had in her collection there. He picked up a book of motivational quotations, and skimmed through the pages, desperately searching for some guidance on how to handle Jannie. Absorbed in his book, he didn't notice Jerry approaching him, until he was standing directly beside him.

"Hello Bill," he boomed. "Nice to see you again. I'm sorry I didn't have a chance to say goodbye properly but..." He shrugged as if to say, 'this is the burden of being such a successful businessman'.

He then asked Bill how he was enjoying South Africa so far. "It's just fine," Bill responded carefully. Jerry casually asked Bill if he'd found any more cards, like the ones he'd described on the plane.

Bill shook his head. "Why are you interested in these cards?" he asked Jerry.

"Oh, I'm not really interested", responded Jerry casually. "I was just making conversation." Jerry's bodyguard began to point at his watch. "I'm sorry, I need to get to an important meeting." He handed Bill his business card. Bill glanced at the card. 'Jerry Khumalo. Director of the Khumalo Group of Companies/for all your transportation and entertainment needs.' "Please feel free to contact me if I can help you in any way while you're here," he offered. Jerry and his escort left the store, leaving Bill to wonder if the visit was planned or sheer coincidence.

The hotel's dining room was crowded. The hotel had a special function on, according to the waiter, and would Bill mind sitting at the table by the window? Bill sat down and ordered some wine. As he sipped his cabernet, he thought about the day's events. He'd felt very uncomfortable about the people he'd met today. Jannie, Vuse and Jerry. They seemed so strange. Jerry was correct. He didn't understand their culture. He wondered how he was going to manage in this strange country. He missed home. He missed his family and friends. Hell, he missed America. What he would only do to hear an American accent.

A short man with a mop of white hair appeared at his table. "I'm sorry to disturb you, but this place is rather full tonight. Would you mind if I sat at your table?" Bill's heart leapt on hearing the Texan drawl. "It would be my pleasure," replied Bill, meaning every word.

Chett Winter, a Texan, was now living in Minneapolis, Minnesota. A retired businessman, he worked as a voluteer for the International Executive Service Corps. Although he'd worked in a number of developing countries on USAID projects, he loved being in South Africa.

"It's a privilege for me to be working in this country. One has a sense of having a unique opportunity to make a real contribution to the development of this society", he explained. "Don't you find the culture a little different?" enquired Bill. "It takes some getting used to," agreed Chett, "but this is my third trip here, and I guess it just grows on you."

Chett suddenly stood up and began waving. A striking blonde woman, dressed in a neon pink silk jacket and black trousers had entered the room. She saw Chett, grinned and bounced towards them.

"I thought I'd never find you, with it being so busy," she sang with an Irish lilt. Bubbly, positive, vivacious, Brenda was the perfect antidote to the Jannies of the world. Talking to her was like being connected to a live power cable filled with positive energy. She'd arrived in South Africa two years ago on a six month contract. The six months kept being extended until she had to admit that she was hooked on the place.

"I used to live in the most beautiful part of Ireland, with rolling green hills, fresh air, wide cobbled streets and all that," she recalled. " I was happy there, until I came to South Africa. At first you don't notice it, but after you've been here a while you discover a special energy here. It's something I can't quite describe. But have you noticed the light in South Africa? Doesn't it seem different from home?"

Bill thought about it and nodded.

"And the people," she continued, "the people here also

seem to vibrate to a different energy..."

Bill was curious: "But don't you miss home?" he asked.

"Of course I do. But the trick here is to get yourself a home from home. For example, where are you staying?" she asked.

"In this hotel," replied Bill.

"That's the first thing you need to sort out. Hotels can be very impersonal. You'll always feel like a stranger in a hotel. I'm going to give you the name of a Bed and Breakfast near here which will make you feel like you're living at home. The lady that runs it, Sandi Marshall, is a wonderfully warm caring person. She is like a mother without the guilt. Before I got my own flat, I used to rush home from work and tell her about my day. She'd pour me a glass of wine and I'd perch on the bar stool watching her cook dinner. I miss her home cooked meals even now..."

Bill smiled at the thought and took down the phone number.

They began chatting about their experiences in South Africa. Chett and Brenda smiled sympathetically as Bill described his time with Jannie and Vuse. "I've also worked with a Jannie type," mused Brenda. "He represents the old South Africa. The Vuses of the world reflect the new South Africa. You have to remember that this country is in the middle of a transformation from an apartheid order to a new democracy. Usually a change of magnitude would be characterised by war, violence, and revenge. The peaceful birth of South Africa was seen as a modern day miracle. But what makes this place so interesting is that it is full of paradoxes. Some people will talk about a nation of grime and crime. For others it is a rainbow nation, full of promise and reconciliation. The only thing I can tell you with certainty is this: South Africa and its people will get into your soul. You won't leave here unaffected."

5 There are no Tigers in Darkest Africa

In a dark time the eye
begins to see

— Theodore Roethke

Bill awoke with a shock to a loud crash. It sounded like someone was trying to get into his room. He held his breath and listened. Sandi's dogs were barking urgently outside. There was another crash. The door shuddered. He sat bolt upright listening to every sound. Were they looking for him? That evening, over a glass of wine, he and Sandi had discussed the horror story that was being spread via the Internet. A Johannesburg businessman had woken up to find two men peering down at him. They'd taken delight in tormenting him for six hours with a hot iron, burning his face, his buttocks and his entire body. When they'd finished, they'd left him for dead. He'd survived, only just. Bill's mind then jumped to the article he'd read on how youths were initiated into gangs. To prove their courage they were required to torture their victims before killing them. Was he being targeted now? The day before, someone had broken into his room and gone through his things. The maid had thought she'd seen a grey BMW idling outside the house, just before the break in. Nothing had been taken, but Sandi was concerned. She'd never had a problem with security since she'd put up the electrified fence around her home. She phoned the security service to find out why her alarm hadn't been activated. The security company had apologised profusely. They couldn't understand why the signal hadn't gone through. They would come out to check the system tomorrow. But that wasn't going to help him now.

He looked at the bedside clock. It was 2.45 a.m. He heard Sandi calling the dogs inside. He listened again. The house was quiet. Whoever had tried to break into his room was gone. All he could hear was the rain outside. He tried to go back to sleep, but his mind kept churning through the events of his first three weeks in Johannesburg.

He hated Johannesburg. He hated the constant fear that stalked him every day. He hated the daily dose of news about violence, crime, fraud and corruption. He hated the way people lived in terror behind their high walls and electrified fences. He hated the poverty, the dirt, and the litter that he saw every day on his way to work. And most of all he hated the beggars hobbling about on fake crutches at every traffic light. They were con artists – just like him. He'd told everyone his mission was to build a centre of excellence in Johannesburg. He laughed at the thought. Who was he fooling? He would never be able to transform the lazy, sullen, resentful workers at Branded Apparel into a motivated, productive team. He felt like he'd been wading through a marshy darkness without a torch, whilst his team at Branded Apparel, kept throwing obstacles in his path. He could hear their gleeful laughter as he stumbled.

And then there was Jannie. From the start Jannie had irritated him. No matter how many times Bill had asked to be called by his name, Jannie insisted on calling him 'boss' in a mocking tone. Then he'd offer to help Bill communicate with the workers. "I understand their culture. I know how to talk to them." Later on Bill would discover what he'd been saying to the workers. "The boss says unless you work harder, you'll lose your jobs," or "The boss says there will be no increases this year for those of you who are disruptive". Now he understood why the workers had fallen silent or looked away when he walked past them. Jannie had been deliberately setting up a barrier of distrust between Bill and his people.

Bill thought he was imagining it at first, but Jannie seemed to be following him around. He'd slide into Bill's office complaining about how lazy the workers were. Or he 'just had to inform Bill that he'd spotted Vuse reading the new Employment Equity Act which just proved he was trying to find a way to get rid of the whites and force the company to recruit more blacks. Not that he had anything against blacks, or even the new government.'

Bill's head would ache at the constant blaming and complaining that poured out of Jannie's mouth. Once he realised that Jannie was an incurable time waster, Bill tried to avoid him. He kept his office door shut, but that did not stop Jannie from simply barging in whenever he wanted. Bill put his foot down and refused to see Jannie unless they had an appointment. That didn't deter Jannie at all. He'd simply open the door to the office and say "Excuse me, I know you don't want to be disturbed, but this is really important." It never was, of course. Jannie would simply request Bill's permission to buy more tea bags, or ask Bill whether he thought Doris could take sick leave. After a day of constant interruptions, Bill read Jannie the riot act. He informed Jannie that he was not allowed to interrupt Bill when he was meeting with a customer. From now on they would have a weekly meeting to discuss Jannie's problems. Other than that, he did not want to see Jannie near his office.

Jannie stopped his pranks and kept out of Bill's way. Bill heaved a huge sigh of relief. He was busy congratulating himself on having found a way to control Jannie when he received a phone call from the human resources director of Fedics. Fedics was one of Branded Apparel's most important clients.

"When can I expect my order to be delivered?" asked Charles.

"What order is this?" asked Bill.

He heard the irritation in Charles' voice. "Two months ago, I ordered 500 T-shirts for a special launch which is taking place next week. Mr Engelbrecht promised it would be delivered two weeks ago. When I phoned to follow up, he assured us the order would be ready by Monday. He'd said that you were seeing to it personally.

Now I don't know what is happening in your company, and I don't care. If we don't have our order by the end of this week, you can consider it cancelled." Bill apologised profusely and promised to sort it out right away.

He strode to Jannie's desk and demanded an explaination.

Jannie's defiant response enraged Bill: "Excuse me boss, but I wanted to tell you about Fedics. You said you didn't want to be interrupted, no matter how important it was. So I was waiting for our next meeting on Monday to inform you we had a problem."

Bill found himself trembling with anger. He was ready to fire Jannie on the spot. Before Bill could say a word, Jannie had disappeared. Within a minute Jannie had reappeared carrying another of his interminable manuals. Bill couldn't believe the man's impudence.

"Vuse is mobilising the workers against management again." Jannie spoke as though nothing had happened. "You'd better read this new Labour Relations Act before we dismiss him, otherwise we could land up in industrial court." He flew out the office before Bill could explode.

"That's it," thought Bill. "You're fired."

As Bill skimmed through the Labour Relations Act, a flash of insight pierced through his anger. "The sneaky bastard," he thought, "this has nothing to do with Vuse at all. Jannie knew I was about to fire him. He's warning me against even trying." He read through the entire act again and slammed the book down on the table. Jannie was safe. The Labour Relations Act protected Jannie from dismissal, unless he was caught in the act of theft, sabotage, or fraud. And Jannie was too sly to be caught doing anything. The master of deception merely spun webs of innuendo, half truths and subtle lies. There was nothing Bill could ever prove in a court of law. Jannie had a reasonable excuse for everything.

Branded Apparel had been operating on excuses and broken promises for far too long. It was time for him to take control. He needed to sort out the Fedics mess now. Who could he rely on to get things done? He suddenly caught sight of a short, stocky figure speaking to Doris.

"Koos," he called. "I need you in my office now!" As Koos walked into his office, he could see Jannie smirking. Koos sat down quietly and listened as Bill explained what had happened with Fedics.

"What will it take to get the job done by Friday?" Bill asked.

Koos was silent for a minute. "It's almost impossible," he finally answered. "With overtime I could get it done by Tuesday, but the staff aren't going to be happy. You're going to have to explain it to them."

Bill looked at the relaxed group in front of him. Jannie was missing. Vuse and Nandi were laughing at a joke. With his mouth full of gum, Jay was looking at Bill curiously. Doris was coughing out the remnants of her flu. Rosalie was sitting quietly alone.

"We have a major problem facing us right now," announced Bill as he dropped the bombshell.

"We were supposed to have 500 T-shirts ready for

Fedics by last week. They've given us till Friday or we lose the account. I'm going to try to negotiate for Tuesday, but if we don't get it right this time we're going to lose one of our biggest customers. I've asked Koos to organise things while I try to do some damage control with Fedics. We're going to need some overtime from you..."

Vuse and Doris began talking in a foreign language. Doris was gesticulating angrily. Rosalie looked sullen. Bill could make out words like *I can't*, *school*, *last minute crisis* and *management*. Soon everyone was shouting and waving their hands around. Bill could no longer hear individual voices above the roar.

Koos stood up holding a clipboard and began to allocate tasks to everyone. He spoke quietly but firmly: "To get this job out by Tuesday, we need to do 100 T-shirts a day, and I need you all here on Saturday. Rosalie, help Nandi with the cutting please. Vuse, help Doris' team with the sewing. Sipho, you help Johannes do the packing, and the rest of you will do your normal jobs. We go home when we've hit the 100 mark."

Everyone began shouting at once. Bill could still hear the uproar as he opened his car door.

Charles at Fedics was not happy when Bill asked for extra time to complete the job: "I don't appreciate being messed around by you people. Every week you tell me my order will be ready next week, and it isn't. I have a launch on Friday. I need those T-shirts. If it weren't too late to give it to someone else I would have cancelled our order weeks ago. You have until Tuesday. If you don't get those

T-shirts to me by then, Fedics will never do business with you again."

Jannie was hovering around Bill's office when he returned. Bill ignored him. Koos peered in. "I'm sorry to interrupt you, but I need to fill you in on what is happening with the Fedics job," he said. "I was checking our supplies today and found out that we have only enough material for 300 T-shirts. Jannie ordered more material, but for some reason the order didn't go through. We've tried all over, but no-one can help us in such a short space of time. If we don't get the material within two days we're going to be in trouble. I have a few more suppliers that I'm going to try today. I'll let you know what happens."

Bill listened without a word. It was strange. He felt totally calm. He knew what he had to do, Labour Relations Act or not. Jannie had been sabotaging him from the day he'd arrived.

He didn't seem surprised when Bill called him into his office and fired him. Bill had expected Jannie to argue, or threaten him. But his quiet reaction left Bill feeling unsettled. Bill didn't trust him. It was obvious he was plotting something. If only Bill could discover what it was, he could avoid another Fedics disaster. He called in Koos and asked for a list of every customer, past and present of Branded Apparel. During the next two weeks he would visit every one of them, and counteract any little schemes Jannie had up his sleeve.

The factory was humming with activity. He could hear the clicking of scissors, the whine of sewing machines and the scrunching of plastic as Johannes stuffed the completed T-shirts into their packets. Every now and then he'd hear an angry voice rising above the buzz. He couldn't understand the language, but he could see his people were not impressed with having to work overtime.

"Well," he thought as he rushed off to see Foschini, "they're just going to have to get used to it." He'd watched them drifting around for weeks now, and it was time they developed some discipline. They just didn't seem to realise that the factory and their jobs were at stake.

The rot in the Johannesburg operations was far worse than he could ever have imagined. Bill had spent three days listening to an avalanche of complaints about late deliveries, shoddy merchandise, and constant broken promises. Every customer he met had either stopped doing business with Branded Apparel, or was giving them one last chance. There was not one single customer he'd met that had a good word to say about Branded Apparel. Small wonder they hadn't been making any profits. The final insult came when the quality control manager of Edgars had held up one of their shirts and declared: "The only good thing that came out of our dealings with Branded Apparel is this shirt." He pointed to the buttons, the seams, the collar, and a flaw in the material. "We use this on our training courses as an example of exceptionally poor quality."

Bill sighed as he thought of the huge mountain that had to be conquered before he could even begin to dream of fulfilling his mission. It was obvious that there was little if any discipline or system in the factory. Productivity was downright awful. His first step was to get the factory working efficiently again. Then he had the momentous task of trying to win back the trust of their customers. Only after that could he consider building his centre of excellence. He was running out of time. Three weeks had passed. He had less than six months left. There was so much to be done, and so little time.

It was not a good time to find his workers dancing and singing in the street outside the factory. As he parked his car, Koos came rushing towards him. "What is going on?" asked Bill. "We have a deadline to meet." Koos shrugged his shoulders hopelessly "They're on strike. I've tried everything I can to get them back to work, but they won't listen." Something inside of Bill snapped. "Like hell they won't," he seethed. After putting his reputation on the line, he was not going to miss Tuesday's deadline for anything. There was no way he was going to give Jannie the satisfaction of watching him fail.

As he strode towards them they began singing louder, and dancing towards him, blocking his path to the factory. "What is going on here?" demanded Bill, "we have a deadline to meet. Get back to work immediately!"

The crowd continued singing defiantly. Bill was furious. He tried unsuccessfully to shove his way through the swaying wall. Suddenly Vuse appeared in front of him. The crowd quietened down.

"What are you doing?" demanded Bill. "We have a

deadline to meet."

"We won't go back to work until our demands are met," declared Vuse.

Bill couldn't believe they had the gall to be making demands. After what he'd heard from his customers, they were lucky to keep their jobs. "What demands are those?" he enquired contemptuously.

Vuse's words astounded him: "We want Jannie back. We want Koos fired. And we want Friday afternoons off like the other factories. And we want overtime pay."

Bill was puzzled. Why on earth would they want slimy Jannie back? It was obvious he hated them. Bill had seen him insult them to their faces. An image of a smirking Jannie back on the job flashed through Bill's mind. He saw a furious Charles from Fedics cancelling the order as Jannie invented another lame excuse for missing the deadline. A chain of angry customers floated in front of his eyes shouting 'More broken promises, more broken promises.' Then he saw Bob, the human resources director of Branded Apparel saying: "I'm sorry Bill, but we expected more from you. You're fired." It was Papas all over again.

The anger within him erupted. "You listen to me. I am in charge here. Not Jannie. I was sent here from the USA to see if this factory is worth saving. My bosses are thinking of closing this factory down and shipping it to Malaysia, where the people want to work. I have spent the last three days listening to our customers who have nothing nice to say about you. Your work is shoddy. Jobs are never completed on time. Some of the stores use our clothes as examples of poor quality on their training courses. They laugh at how bad we are. No one wants to buy our clothes any more. Fedics is giving us one last chance. If we blow this, we'll never get work from them again. We've already lost Edgars, Woolworths, and Foschini. So you guys have a choice to make. If you want to save this factory and keep your jobs we have a lot of work to do. Meeting the deadline on Tuesday is only the beginning. But if you'd rather sing and dance that is fine by me. You can save me a lot of trouble. I will simply go back to the USA and tell them that the South African workers don't want jobs."

The crowd was silent as Bill turned around and strode to his car. He'd had enough for one day. He was going home.

He'd arrived back to find the house empty. What a pity. He needed someone to talk to. Someone that understood him. He phoned Brenda, but her line just rang. He tried Rose, but she was out of town. He thought of Sharon. He wondered how she'd react to his call. It was worth the chance. He dialled her number. A machine answered. He didn't leave a message.

He opened a beer and lay sipping it on his couch. Jerry had been right. He didn't understand these people's culture. Who would have guessed that Jannie would sabotage him like this? Who could have expected the black workers to strike to get their slave master back? This job was turning out to be more than he could handle. So was the country. That night he and Sandi had watched TV together and had discussed the violent crime in South Africa.

He looked at his watch. 5.30 a.m. It had been a long night. He sighed. He didn't want to go to the factory today and face a group of striking workers again. He hated acting the dictator. But he simply had to get the Fedics order out, no matter what. He dragged himself to the bathroom. Time to get ready for another tough day.

"Did you hear the thunder last night?" asked Sandi at breakfast.

"That was thunder?" asked Bill. "I heard a crash and thought someone was trying to break into my room."

She smiled sympathetically. "The thunderstorms we get here can be very frightening. My dogs always go crazy. I hope they didn't keep you awake for too long."

Bill felt embarrassed. It had only been a thunderstorm after all. He looked outside. Things looked so normal in the daylight. 'What is happening to me?' he wondered. He'd lain awake all night gripped by terror for nothing. It was this country. It was getting to him. All the news of violence on television was affecting his psyche. He was beginning to believe South Africa was really a nation overwhelmed by crime. He remembered Brenda's insight about the paradox of South Africa: "A country of grime and crime and yet a rainbow nation of hope." Brenda had such a positive attitude about everything. She saw South Africa as a rainbow nation imbued with a rare energy, and so that is what she experienced. He filled his head with thoughts of negativity and violence. Small wonder he lay awake at night in terror. He realised he would have to work on becoming more positive.

As he drove to work he noticed how everything had been washed clean by the rain. The trees seemed greener. The buildings were brighter. The roads were shinier. A positive feeling surged through him. It was going to be a good day after all.

The factory was already buzzing with activity when he arrived. The busy workers greeted him politely as he walked past. He noticed a number of completed T-shirts stacked in the corner of his office. Jay sauntered into his office his face beaming with accomplishment.

"I've got good news," he announced. "We'll have all the material we need to complete the Fedics order by 10 O'clock today." Jay then proceeded to describe how he'd managed to organise this incredible deal through one of his contacts. "Anything else you need, just ask me," he offered proudly. "I have friends everywhere." Bill pointed to the T-shirts in his office. "Oh that is our first 100 T-shirts for Fedics. We should have the job completed by Monday afternoon." Jay grinned. Bill smiled to himself. It was going to be all right.

It was amazing how suddenly everything had worked out. The impossible challenge of meeting Fedics' deadline had been achieved easily enough. 500 T-shirts were delivered to Fedics at 11 O'clock Tuesday morning. Then on Tuesday afternoon, another opportunity was dangled in front of them.

The purchasing director of a retail fashion chain called Mr Price came to see Bill. "Can you make jackets like this?" he asked, showing Bill a collarless unstructured jacket. Bill took a deep breath and responded. "Sure thing. When do you need them by?"

"I'd like to see a sample by the end of this week. If the quality is right, we'll put in an order for 800 of these to be completed by the end of the month." Bill was ecstatic. Another big contract would improve their figures substantially.

Bill congratulated his team on completing the Fedics order. Then he told them the good news about Mr Price. He was surprised when the usually quiet Rosalie volunteered to design the jacket for Mr Price. She explained that she had been doing a design course at night, and she would love the challenge of putting what she'd learnt into practice. By Friday she'd produced a jacket that was better than the one given to them by Mr Price. They had got the order. For the first time Bill was able to report back a 'success story' to head office.

Fresh from a weekend in the Pilanesberg game reserve with Brenda, Bill felt charged up and ready for the week. He'd instructed Rosalie to show the team how to make up the jackets. Jay was organising the fabric, and Koos was tasked with project managing the job. They were on their way to turning around the factory.

A few hours later, a frustrated Bill watched his team disintegrate. Koos shuffled around most of the day, and went home early, sick with flu. Sullen Nandi seemed to be working at half pace. Vuse appeared quite distracted. Doris seemed to be totally disinterested in what she was doing. She wasn't even looking down at the seam she was sewing. Bill walked over to inspect her work. It was downright sloppy. It would never meet the Mr Price quality standards.

Bill lost his temper: "What is wrong with you?" he shouted. "You're being totally careless with your work. Mr Price is going to send this right back. Take it out and do it again – like this." He grabbed Rosalie's sample and thrust it in front of Doris. He saw a tear forming in Doris' eye. He ignored it and strode away.

From his office he saw the workers swarming around Doris, talking in their strange language again. He suppressed his desire to order them back to work and simply observed them. He watched Doris telling her story. The throng began muttering amongst themselves. Sipho raised his voice and the crowd began shaking their fists angrily. Bill heard a crash, and a sewing machine was thrown to the ground. He wondered what to do. Should he confront them now or wait? Should he call the police? Suddenly he heard Vuse's voice calming them down. He looked like he was promising them something. Each member of the crowd had his say and then he saw them nodding in agreement. Three people emerged from the crowd. Vuse, Doris and Jay asked to talk to Bill.

"The workers have asked us to represent them," began Vuse.

"Please sit down," responded Bill.

"They have given us a mandate to negotiate on their behalf," explained Jay.

Bill listened.

Doris took a deep breath and stumbled over her words. "We the workers have demands. We want overtime for all the extra work we're doing. We want Friday afternoons off like all the other factories get. We want training..."

Bill interrupted her midstream: "I'm sorry, but I simply can't meet your demands. We are barely profitable as it is. If we're going to survive, we are all simply going to have to work a lot harder than ever before."

"But that's unfair," complained Sipho.

A distant memory began to form in Bill's mind. Where had he heard that before? 'It's unfair'. Memories of that dreadful time in his past flashed before his eyes. His firing from Papas. The unfairness of it all. Lawyers. Meetings. Fighting. Struggling. Then he remembered how he'd stumbled across the tiger card, and how its message had finally released him from the cycle of revenge and humiliation… "It doesn't matter if it's fair or not" He found himself murmuring.

Doris muttered something angrily to Vuse about 'umlungu'. Vuse responded in their language.

Then he turned on Bill "You don't care about what is fair, do you? It's always only about business and profits with you. We black people are tired of being oppressed by white management. We deserve more. We had to work overtime to get the Fedics order out on time, but that means nothing to you. Now with the Mr Price job, you expect us to work overtime again. For what? All the other factories get overtime, they get Friday afternoons off…"

Bill heard Vuse's words echoing in the distance. "We deserve more." He pictured himself in the Dickensian bookstore, picking up the tiger card. *You deserve more.* The connections between them and him crystallised into a glorious insight. He was experiencing synchronicity again. On a different continent, a bunch of African workers were going through the lessons of the tiger in their own way. What did this mean? He wondered. He remembered how Rose had suggested that his special purpose was waiting for him in Africa. What if these people shared a common destiny with him?

"You just said that you deserve more," mused Bill.

Vuse looked defensive. "We do deserve more. If you're not prepared to meet our demands then we'll..."

"No, no," interrupted Bill, "I agree with you. You do deserve more. You deserve a lot more than you could possibly imagine right now. I'm sorry I appeared distracted. Believe me. I'm on your side. We just need to find a way..." he mumbled incoherently.

Doris looked confused. 'What sort of a trick is this,' she wondered. She decided to repeat their mandate: "We demand Friday afternoons off, overtime pay, training, and a review of our wages."

Bill remained silent for a while. Finally he spoke. They listened as a voice from deep within him found expression.

"You were quite right to say you deserve more. You do

deserve more. We all deserve more. I deserve more from you and Branded Apparel deserves more from all of us. How we are going to achieve all of this together is beyond me right now. But I believe we owe it to ourselves to find a better way. A way in which we can help each other to get what we deserve."

They looked at him strangely. It wasn't what they'd expected to hear.

"I want to invite you all to come on a journey with me. Together we will explore different ways to get more. I promise to help you on your journeys, if you will help me and the company in return."

Jay broke the spell. "We're not interested in fancy words. Give us something we can take back to the workers. Give us Friday afternoons off. Give us training. Give us overtime."

Bill turned to Vuse who was deep in thought. "The reason none of us are getting what we deserve is because we aren't working together to help each other. You don't trust me, and I don't trust you. We don't trust each other because we don't know each other." Vuse nodded in agreement.

The spring in Bill bubbled; "Not only don't we know one another, but often we don't even know ourselves. I believe our journeys are intertwined. I know that if I don't understand who I am, I can't give myself fully to you. I also know that if you don't discover the power within you, you can't give yourselves fully to the company. It becomes a lose-lose situation. I recently began my own personal journey of self-discovery. This has been an incredible experience for me. So what I'm offering you is the same opportunity that I had. We'll use our Friday afternoons not to work, and not to go home. We'll use them to get to know one another better, and then to find ways to help each other to get what we want."

Vuse looked at Bill thoughtfully. "You're not like any manager we've ever had before. We're going to need to take this back to the workers. I'm not sure how I'm going to explain this to them."

Bill watched Vuse reporting back to the workers. Everyone had a question to ask, and Vuse patiently answered them one by one. At 4.30 p.m. Vuse stepped into his office. "I've spoken to the workers. They're not sure if they can really trust you yet," he grinned, "but they have agreed to give our Friday meetings a chance."

"Thank you," smiled Bill as he offered Vuse a beer. "It can't have been easy to convince them. I appreciate your help in this."

"What are you going to say at the first meeting?" asked Vuse.

"I have no idea," replied Bill earnestly.

"I guess I'm going to have to help you," smiled Vuse. "There is a lot you'll need to understand about our culture if you want to even begin to achieve what I think you are hinting at."

It was 8 O'clock by the time Bill and Vuse reluctantly left the factory. Over a few beers they had found themselves chatting about sports, their families and their past.

Vuse spoke about his father, a simple gardener who had taught him so much about the meaning of life. Bill spoke about his grandmother, the story teller, whose characters always directed him out of any predicament. Vuse shared some of the experiences he'd had as a trade unionist. Bill spoke about his time with Papas, and the voyage of discovery that had brought him to Africa. Vuse was delighted to hear about the tiger cards. "That's the American version of our sangoma," he declared. Bill in turn learnt about the old mystical African women who could foretell the future by throwing the bones. Vuse offered to introduce him to a sangoma sometime. Bill promised to bring in the tiger cards. As they shared the last beer, they agreed to meet after work the next day to plan in detail their Friday meeting.

Bill arrived home to find Brenda waiting impatiently for him. "Where have you been? I've been waiting for ages. I couldn't wait to get here to show you something you are going to just love. I couldn't believe it when one of my delegates gave me this card. Is this one of yours?"

He grabbed the familiar purple card, eagerly anticipating its wisdom.

polish away the grime
to reveal the shine

"It is," he grinned. "Thanks. It's just what I need."

"What does it mean?" she asked.

"I have no idea. But I guess I'm about to find out."

He felt charged up. It was all going to work out. The force was back with him.

The next day the factory was buzzing with energy. Above the whine of the sewing machines, voices could be heard asking questions. Every now and then Vuse's reassuring answer would be heard. The factory had never had a meeting like this before. The staff were both nervous and excited about participating.

Bill couldn't wait to show Vuse the tiger card he'd got from Brenda. As they sipped their beer that evening, he took the card out and put it in front of Vuse.

"My American sangoma came to me last night with this message. What do you think it means?"

Vuse read the card silently. He looked like he was in a deep trance. Finally he spoke.

"The grime is our past. It is the pain of apartheid. A time when we were separated as a people. Separated from one another, and separated from our very nature. Only by working through our pain will we restore our natural ubuntu. Our souls. Our pure way of being. Our trust and inner harmony."

They were both silent as they tried to imagine the task ahead.

The door opened and Jay walked in. "Sorry to interrupt you so late, but I need you to sign this order form for me before I go." Bill felt irritated. Jay's interruption had broken the spell. While he was signing the form, he noticed Jay staring curiously at the card and at Vuse. Bill ignored his unspoken question.

When Jay had left, they tried to reconnect to the special energy that had made everything seem so clear. But it was gone.

Finally Vuse asked: "What does polishing away the grime mean to you Bill?"

Bill didn't feel inspired, but struggled through an answer. "I'm not sure. But the image that comes into my mind is polishing tarnished brass. Two years ago, Sharon and I restored an old house, and I remember trying to polish up the door nobs. I had to use a soft cloth to ensure I didn't scratch the metal. Then I had to polish vigorously. For a long time it seemed like I was making no progress at all. As the tarnish loosened, it seemed that all I was doing was moving the grime around. Finally just as I was about to give up, the brass began to shine through. It made a big difference to our house," he added. "It made it seem so much brighter." He sighed nostalgically as he thought of his old home.

"That's it," whispered Vuse. "That is what we're going to have to do."

"What is that?" asked Bill.

"If we want to win the trust of the people. If we want to help them restore their humanity. If we want to create a spirit of ubuntu in this factory, we are going to have to polish away a lot of pain, distrust, disappointment and even bitterness. That is going to be a long, messy business. I hope we have the stomach for it."

Throughout Friday, a feeling of excitement pulsated through the factory. This was the first time that every worker, regardless of rank was part of a meeting of this nature. At 2 O'clock Vuse cleared an area in the centre of the factory. Doris began herding everyone to the meeting area where Vuse sent them right back. They needed to bring their own chairs. Much muttering was heard as people with chairs tried to pass those moving in the other direction. Those seated were shouting to their friends to join them. People were lifting chairs over one another, whilst Sipho was trying to get them to move closer to one another to make room for the others. It was pandemonium all around.

Bill and Vuse were standing in front of the group, talking quietly to one another. "This is it," whispered Vuse. "Time to begin polishing."

Vuse called the group to order. "Today we begin a new era at Branded Apparel. A time where we the workers, join hands with management to find a better way for all of us. I'd like to call on our leader Bill to explain what we're going to do."

Bill stood up and faced the silent audience. He paused, trying to form a sentence out of the words tumbling inside his brain. "At the moment we are all dissatisfied with the way things are at Branded Apparel. You believe you deserve more than what you are getting. I believe this company can be far greater than what it is today. The purpose of our Friday sessions is to provide a forum in which we can all get to know one another better. Together we are going to find solutions to problems we see at the factory. At these meetings we can discuss anything. What is working for us. What isn't working. What we'd like to do differently. What would make this factory a better place for us all. So I'd like to ask you to talk to me. What would you like to see change in this company?"

Bill looked at the group. Eighty people were watching him silently. He waited. He heard shuffling. Someone coughed. He looked around for someone to answer him. Everyone was avoiding his eyes. The silence became unbearable. Bill turned to Doris.

"What would you like this company to do, Doris?" he asked.

Doris looked embarrassed. She shifted in her chair, and then looked around the room. Bill kept quiet.

Finally, Doris responded hesitantly: "We want training."

Bill heaved a sigh of relief. "What sort of training do you want?" he asked gently. Again there was silence.

Doris seemed to be struggling to articulate her thoughts. "We want training to be better in our jobs," she finally answered. Bill wanted to hear something more specific, but decided against asking her again. She was clearly uncomfortable speaking in front of the group.

Bill waited. Nandi pushed her braided hair back and stood up. "We want overtime pay," she said defiantly and sat down. The group was silent once more. Someone coughed. Everyone looked around. A large black woman at the back put her hand up. "Yes?" encouraged Bill. "What do you want to see?"

"What about maternity leave?" she demanded.

Bill was confused. This wasn't going the way he'd expected. What could he say to bring the discussion back on track? He thought of the special energy he and Vuse had shared when they had discussed the meaning of the tiger card. How could he infuse that kind of energy into this group? His thoughts were interrupted by Sipho who was standing in front of the group.

"We want more pay," he shouted. Everyone nodded in agreement. "We want overtime."

Like a preacher, he waited for the response. "Yes, we want overtime, we want transparency."

An echo came from the group: "We want transparency." He had the audience in the palm of his hands. "We want democracy!" The group sang their approval. "We want democracy!"

"We want transformation!" A few people stood up and began to dance. "We want transformation! We want transformation!"

The meeting was getting out of control.

Vuse caught Bill's eye and quickly intervened. "Thank you, Sipho, for those inspirational words."

An awkward silence descended on the group. The dancers sat down. Vuse looked around as the group quietened down. "I think the next step for us is to decide how we should go about getting the transformation we want."

Sipho, wanting to get his audience back, stood up and shouted "We want a transformation steering committee!"

"Good idea," said Vuse, retaining control of the group.

"Who should represent us on the committee?" For the next 20 minutes the group debated the composition of the committee. Finally seven names were agreed upon by the group: Vuse, Doris, Sipho, Jay, Nandi, Koos and Rosalie were given a mandate to meet with Bill on a weekly basis to manage a transformation process within Branded Apparel. The committee was required to report back to the main group after each meeting.

At 4.30 p.m. people started looking at their watches. Vuse closed the meeting. "I believe we have made an excellent start to our transformation process," he declared. "Thank you for your contribution. On behalf of the transformation committee we would like to thank you for the trust you have placed in us, and we assure you we will do our best for you."

Bill watched in confusion as the group noisily packed their chairs away and departed. A number of people came up to Vuse and shook his hand. The six representatives of the new steering committee stayed behind. Vuse shook each of their hands in turn. Then he addressed them. "Congratulations on your nomination. We have an important task ahead of us. Our first meeting is next Friday at 2 O'clock in Bill's office."

Vuse walked Bill out to his car. "What happened there?" asked Bill. "At one stage I thought we were losing them." Vuse grinned. "Me too. Sipho sure had them going. But it turned out OK. We now have a small group we can work with. And our committee has a mandate to act on behalf of the entire factory."

The following week Bill noticed a different atmosphere in the factory. Everyone seemed more outgoing and more relaxed. Staff members whose names Bill barely knew, were suddenly greeting him as he walked passed. The members of the transformation steering committee seemed to have acquired an elevated status amongst the workers. Bill smiled to himself as he caught Doris criticising Thandi over the quality of a seam. When Sipho was exhorting a group of workers not to waste time after tea, because 'by harming the factory they were harming themselves.' Bill caught Vuse winking at him.

The members of the transformation steering committee arrived at their first meeting in Bill's office, filled with expectations. A wave of adrenaline shot through Bill as he looked at the six people seated in the circle. His fate, and the future of Branded Apparel lay in the hands of this committee. He took a deep breath and began by thanking the group for the important role he knew they were going to play.

"Today is a very important day for all of us. In our hands lies the future of Branded Apparel and all its people. Our purpose is to find a way to allow both the company and its people to reach their full potential. I'm now going to open this to the floor. What do you think our first step should be?"

Each member of the team had a different response. Doris wanted to talk about training. Sipho thought the committee should discuss affirmative action. Koos was concerned about job security. Rosalie wanted to talk about designing a new range for Branded Apparel. Jay thought they should discuss the new Employment Equity legislation. The discussion went around in circles, until finally Sipho asked the group what they thought their mandate was.

Bill listened as empty rhetoric filled the air.

"We are here to achieve transformation!"

"What about transparency. Without transparency there can be no trust!"

"We need to ensure there is empowerment too. What is political empowerment without economic empowerment?" He felt disappointed. They were getting nowhere fast. He thought of the card: *polish away the grime to reveal the shine*. They had barely begun removing the dirt.

Suddenly he heard Vuse addressing him: "How do you see your mandate Bill?"

Bill thought for a while and then slowly answered: "I have three mandates to fill: A mandate to myself; a mandate to you, the workers of Branded Apparel; and a mandate to the company. My mandate to myself is to become someone I can be proud of." He hesitated as he tried to put his emotions into words. "In my past, I was trying so hard to be what I thought others wanted me to be that I lost myself… I became a person I didn't like." He paused, thinking about the end of Papas.

"And now, what I want is... I guess I want to be more like my grandmother." He looked around. They were staring at him in surprise. As he pictured his grandmother, the words tumbled out. "My grandmother was a special lady. When I was a child, she used to tell me stories. I remember how she once told me that everyone is both the author and the hero in the story of his own life. Each day we write a few paragraphs. Over time our paragraphs become chapters, and our chapters become our lives. She would always ask me if I was writing my story the way I wanted my life to be..." He stared wistfully at his past, then smiled. " ... She's dead now, but today I would like to be able to say to her that I'm working on a chapter that describes how I and a group of special people are creating a unique kind of factory. A factory where people help each other to learn and to grow."

Vuse smiled and picked up on the energy. "My hero was my father. He was a poor man. A gardener. But he believed in me. He made me feel that I could accomplish anything. I would like to give that same gift to all our people at the factory. A feeling they can be anything they want to be."

He looked at Doris. Doris spoke about her mother, a domestic who had taught her to be proud of everything she did in life. "I haven't thought about her for a long time," she said wistfully.

A current of positive energy encircled the group as each team member described a special person in their lives. As they shared their stories about their personal heroes, they felt connected by a unique purpose. A purpose that was difficult to describe in words. They were somehow going to share this special energy they were experiencing with the rest of the factory.

Bill walked to his car deep in thought. It had been a long week but he was feeling full of energy. Something magical had happened in his team as they were sharing their stories. How could he describe it? The words 'trust', 'bond', 'sharing,' and 'caring' came to mind. It had happened quicker than he'd expected but a little bit of brass was already shining through. He remembered how surprised the team had been when Koos and Vuse had shared such similar stories of growing up poor. Some things, like poverty and hope, aren't bounded by race he observed.

Deep in thought he didn't notice them approaching until he was rudely shoved from behind. As he fell to the ground he was aware of someone grabbing his briefcase and running away. 'I'm being mugged,' He thought. He heard the sound of an engine starting up. Before he could get up, he saw a grey BMW speeding away.

Vuse came running towards him. "Are you alright?" he asked urgently.

In a daze Bill answered: "I'm fine, but they took my briefcase."

"Was there anything valuable in it?" demanded Vuse.

"No, I have my wallet in my pocket. There were just some notes and the sangoma card, that's all." Vuse looked concerned. He looked around cautiously, and then insisted on walking Bill right to his car.

The shock didn't hit Bill at first. He was fine driving home. He was even casual about it when he told Sandi he'd been mugged. But later that night he began to feel very vulnerable. He found himself shivering. He jumped whenever he heard a strange noise. His mind kept replaying the scene in which he'd been mugged. Why hadn't he fought back? Why had he let them take the briefcase? Why hadn't he been more aware of what was happening around him? He had been warned about the crime situation over and over again. Why hadn't he taken better care? Another voice inside him was less harsh. It had all happened so fast. There was no way he could have seen them coming.

He found himself becoming angry. It wasn't just the fact that they had stolen his briefcase. Worse than that, they had stolen his sense of security. He wasn't safe walking to his car any longer. He wasn't even safe at home. He wasn't safe in this country at all. It was a country of crime and grime after all.

He thought about the grey BMW he'd seen roaring away. It was the key to it all. Sandi's maid had also seen a grey BMW the day they broke into his room. What was going on? Was he being targeted? What was going to happen next? The terror returned.

The next day, the workers were very sympathetic towards Bill. Each one in turn asked him how he was, and commented on how sorry they were about what had happened to him. Bill noticed that neither Vuse nor Jay had come in.

At 10.30 a.m. Vuse strode in and insisted on speaking to Bill privately: "I was worried about you last night. We have never had anyone mugged outside our factory before. So I've spent last night and this morning talking to people about what happened to you. This is what I found out. They are not after you. They want your American sangoma cards."

Bill's eyes widened.

"You'd better sit down. It's a very strange story." Vuse steered Bill towards a chair.

"Before I begin, you are going to need some background about our country. As you know South Africa is in a critical stage of transformation. Only six years ago we were ruled by a repressive apartheid regime which controlled everyone and everything. People were told where they could live, where they could work, what schools their children could go to, and even what they were allowed to read. In 1994 South Africa held its first democratic elections. Everyone was ecstatic. Everyone was free. The rainbow nation was born. The new government began dismantling all the old apartheid legislation and structures that had repressed our people for so long. They also began to empower the previously disadvantaged people of our country. Now imagine this. A country that had been isolated from the world for decades is suddenly thrown open. Investors, tourists, and international aid organisations begin flowing into the country. South African companies suddenly find themselves competing with global players in their own markets. International crime syndicates and drug lords creep in. Illegal immigrants flood in from neighbouring countries seeking a better life. Suddenly our new government is faced with Aids, unemployment, housing, health, and crime problems. Freedom is not easy for people who are not prepared for it. Nor is democracy. Solving all our problems requires an incredible transformation. From disadvantaged to empowered, from crime to crime free, from apartheid to democracy, from poor to prosperous, from unemployment to job creation, from unprofitable to globally competitive...the list is endless. Every government department, municipality, state organisation, business and school in South Africa is involved in some sort of transformation process. And yet people are becoming disheartened by the lack of results. It's been four years since the election, and we don't seem to have been able to solve any of our problems. No one seems to have been able to make transformation work. I believe the person who finds a way to truly manage transformation, will have power beyond their wildest dreams."

Bill looked at Vuse in bewilderment. "So what does this have to do with my being mugged?"

Vuse took out a newspaper clipping and handed it to Bill. "I think you should read this - it appeared in a local newspaper in January this year."

'A small consultancy in Johannesburg claims to have discovered the secret to personal and organisational transformation. Their ten transformation cards have received the attention of the state president, who has asked for a copy of their cards.'

Bill looked up at Vuse. "These are my tiger cards, aren't they?"

Vuse simply nodded. "The cards never made it to the president. No one ever heard of the cards or the consultancy again – until you came along."

"Are you telling me that no one has the full set of these cards?"

Vuse nodded.

"My contacts tell me that the person who finds the full set is either going to be very powerful or very dead."

6 Clearing the Path

It is extraordinary how extraordinary the ordinary person is!

— George Will

"I remember the night I was caught without my pass. As a black you weren't allowed out at night unless you had a dompas. The policeman wouldn't listen that my pass was at home. He hit me on the head and threw me into the back of a truck. And then, and then, he..."

Doris began sobbing. The group was silent. Doris had never spoken of such things before. No one quite knew how to comfort her. The group looked awkward as Doris sat down dabbing her eyes. Vuse reached across and put his hand on hers.

Nandi stood up. She shook slightly as she began telling her story: "We were a family that grew up on laughter. We laughed at everything. When my mom's cooking didn't turn out right, we laughed. When part of our house fell down, we laughed. I remember the day my older brother was taken away to prison. He'd been doing his articles for a law firm that defended black people. They thought he was political. He shouted to me as he was being bundled into the van, 'Tell them, the police have got me.' I didn't know what to do. So I simply laughed. My brother was convicted of high treason and sentenced to 20 years in jail. They beat him up there. We wanted to cry when we saw him, but my brother would say to us, 'Put your tears back. Do not make my enemies happy.' So we would laugh in front of the white people. We wouldn't let them know how much they were hurting us. One day they phoned my parents to say he was dead. He had a heart attack. My brother was strong. We don't know what they did to him in there. No one will tell us. Not even now. Our family doesn't laugh anymore."

No one spoke. A single word would snap the web of trust that was being woven from the shared pain.

Jay stood up. He cleared his voice and began nervously: "We lived in a squatter camp near a river. Every time the river flooded we lost our homes. Mr Khan looked after the camps. Everyone paid him R10 per month to keep out the bad elements. He was talking to the Housing Association about building new houses for the community. Everyone was excited because they were going to get real homes at last. One day the people came from another area. They accused him of being a warlord. They said he'd been stealing money from his own people. They necklaced him. He was my father."

Nandi reached out and touched Jay's hand as he sat down. Bill struggled to control his own emotions. He felt the horror and pain of their stories filling his heart, his lungs and his entire body. Their story had become his story. Their pain was his pain. He felt a tear pricking his eye. He quickly wiped it away.

Vuse began his story: "I started out in a family of six. I'm the fifth born. We were very poor. My parents were illiterate. My father was a gardener. My mother worked as a domestic servant for a white family. I had dreams of becoming educated, going to university, and becoming a Mandela. But I knew my family couldn't provide. Still I studied hard and got my matric. I remember the day I got the forms from the university. I filled them in and I got accepted. But I had so many problems to overcome. We couldn't even afford transport money. The university said there was no accommodation for me. I was scared to go, but my father encouraged me. I'll never forget his words. He said to me: 'As a human being, you have an inherent potential to become something great. Step into the unknown and if you do that, you will discover things you cannot even imagine now.' So I went. Someone gave me money for transport. Then at the university I met someone who helped me to get a loan. I found accommodation. I couldn't afford books, so I spent all my time in the library. After a while they began to call me 'Mr. Library.' Because that is where they could always find me. I eventually passed all my subjects and I got a bursary. Today I wish my parents were alive. I would like to be able to say thank you to them for always believing in me."

The mood of the group lifted. Before them stood a humble hero who had had to overcome many obstacles. Vuse's achievements restored their sense of hope. Before

Vuse could sit down, Sipho jumped up and announced with pride. "What Mr Library didn't mention is that he hasn't given up his books. He is doing his masters in psychology right now." He pumped Vuse's hand. Vuse beamed.

It was time for the next story. No one stood up. Everyone looked at Koos. He began sweating. He slowly rose and stood in front of the group. He opened his mouth as if to begin. "I… I," he stuttered. His face looked grey and strained. He sighed. The group looked at him sympathetically, willing him on. "I was in the army doing my national service. I was posted to the border. We were fighting a war. One day we were told to raid this camp in Angola."

The group watched in fascination as beads of sweat began forming on Koos' brow. He gasped for air. The group stared at him anticipating the horror that was about to be revealed.

"I was feeling sick that night but I was forced to go. I had no choice. I told the captain I was ill, but he screamed abuse at me. We were fighting a war, you see. At the camp, there was confusion." Again he paused, struggling to articulate the nightmare.

"Women were screaming. Shells were going off. I saw things that I still can't talk about... I don't sleep well anymore..." Vuse helped the crumpled man back to his seat.

Bill looked at the group around him in admiration. His mind couldn't cope with the horror of what these people had been forced to experience in their lives. And yet, everyday, they came to work and acted normally. He suddenly felt weary and sore inside. As each story had been told, he'd been absorbing all their pain. He couldn't cope with much more. He noticed Rosalie had stood up and had begun speaking softly.

"In our family abuse of women was natural. My father used to beat my mother regularly. So when I got married and Piet hit me I knew I couldn't complain to my mother. That was the way things were in our community. I always knew I deserved better. But I had nowhere to go. So I accepted that this would be my life. Until the day Piet beat me up so badly that I nearly died... I was pregnant at the time. I lost the baby. That was the turning point for me. It was not easy to leave. My parents refused to help me. I belonged to Piet', they said. 'Who did I think I was acting all superior?' No one would help me. Eventually Jannie agreed to give me a job here. Without it, I wouldn't have been able to survive..."

'So Jannie had a good side after all,' mused Bill. He now understood why the workers had wanted him back.

For a moment, Bill wondered if he'd made an error in firing Jannie. He looked up. Sipho had taken the stage: "Everyone was always proud of my sister. She was the educated one in our family – a teacher. Three months ago she told me she had HIV. I wanted to tell my parents but she wouldn't let me. She was scared what people would say. In our community we believed that only people that slept around got HIV. Only people that deserved it got HIV. She didn't want people to think she was like that. I watched as my beautiful sister became sicker each day. Still we couldn't tell anyone the truth. We went to the library and read every book on terminal diseases we could, in order to find a disease we could tell people she had. We finally chose Hepatitis as it has similar symptoms to Aids. We heard of a clinic that was doing trials on a new anti-aids drug. My sister began her treatment last month and today I heard..." the tears streamed down his face, "today I heard that her cell count has dropped to acceptable levels. She will even be able to have children in the future..."

Everyone was crying and hugging one another. Bill noticed the tears trickling down his own face. He'd never expected the session to turn out quite like this. He'd begun the meeting by suggesting that if they were to trust each other, they needed to know more about each other. So, he'd started by telling them his story of how he'd landed up in South Africa. He'd noticed Doris nodding sympathetically when he'd spoken about how Sharon and Brad had left him. Then Doris had shared her story, and suddenly everything had changed.

He looked at each member of his team in admiration. He couldn't quite believe what each of them had had to overcome in their lives. They were a very special bunch indeed. He felt very close to them right now.

He couldn't get their stories out of his mind. As he drove home, he imagined Doris pleading in the back of the caspir. What had the beasts done to her? What horrors had Koos witnessed in Angola that haunted him so badly? Had Nandi's brother been murdered in prison? How old was Jay when he witnessed his father being set alight? He felt himself gasping for breath. An unbearable pain seized his heart. He tried to focus on the car in front of him. A white Mercedes. The driver, a blonde woman in her thirties was flirting with someone on a mobile phone. Bill watched her blowing a kiss into the phone. He felt strangely disconnected from this 'normal world'.

He arrived home, without knowing how he got there. He hoped Sandi was home. He needed to talk through what he was feeling with someone. But Sandi had gone to movies. Brenda's cheerful voice on the answering machine seemed out of place with what he'd just experienced. He felt vulnerable and lonely. He wondered if he should phone Sharon. But he felt angry with her right now. She'd hurt him with her betrayal. She'd broken up their family. She'd left him for another man and taken Brad. They wouldn't care how he was feeling right now. No one cared about him now he thought bitterly.

His dreams were filled with images of war and violence. He awoke feeling awful. His head throbbed. His heart felt raw, scraped of all emotion. The muscles in his body were aching with pain. He felt like a piece of sodden debris, lying in the wake of a hurricane.

He dragged himself to the bathroom. He didn't want to face the group today. He wondered how he should treat them – knowing what he now knew about them. How would they treat him? He couldn't simply act normally towards them after the experience of the day before. He used to think of this bunch of people as simply workers – whose personal lives were of no relevance to him or to the company. But now Doris, Vuse, Rosalie, Koos, Jay, Nandi and Sipho had become far more than that. Their shared pain had bonded them together. Their shared stories had united them into a common destiny.

Doris was already bending over her sewing machine when Bill walked up the stairs. Bill asked her how she was.

"Fine thank you, and you?"

"Fine thank you," he answered. He was about to say something more, but stopped. Doris returned to her sewing. He walked to his office and began returning his calls.

It was as if nothing had happened. No one spoke about what they had shared the day before. It was back to normal. Bill went out to see the buying manager of Mr Price, who congratulated him on the quality of their jackets, and placed an order for an additional 500. He told the team the good news. They seemed pleased for him. But why were they all so subdued he wondered.

As the week progressed, Bill became concerned about his team. Koos booked in sick with flu. Doris was polite to everyone, but focused all her attention on her work. Jay seemed quite listless. Rosalie had lost all her enthusiasm. She wasn't even excited when Bill had publicly congratulated her for her jacket design that had won the additional Mr Price order. Even Sipho had stopped his usual banter. Bill felt uneasy. A month ago he'd have done anything to trade his unruly bunch of workers for a quiet, efficient team, totally focused on their work. But now he found himself missing the noise, the joking and even the complaining. It was as though all the spirit had been sucked out of the factory. In its place, were a bunch of workers devoid of all emotion.

Then Vuse suggested they postpone the next transformation meeting. Rosalie couldn't make it because she had an exam. Koos was still sick. Doris, Sipho and Jay felt they needed the time to work on the Mr Price order. Everyone had an excuse. Bill was relieved. He didn't think he could handle another emotional session again.

The following week depression sank in. It took all of Bill's willpower to drag himself to the factory every day. He couldn't understand why he was feeling so demotivated. Everything seemed like such an effort. He didn't want to see customers. He didn't want to get any new orders. He didn't want to hear about problems with sourcing materials. He even found himself avoiding Brenda. He couldn't cope with all her enthusiasm right now. He just didn't have the energy for that.

Bill sighed as he checked his email. He wondered how to respond to the cheerful email from head office which asked him how he was doing with regard to creating a centre of excellence in Africa. He couldn't tell them that simply surviving each day took everything out of him. 'It is strange,' he thought. 'I haven't thought about my mission for a long time.'

Vuse interrupted his thoughts. "The team wants to cancel the transformation meeting again this week. They need the time to complete the Mr Price order."

"Don't worry. I can use the extra time myself."

Vuse looked concerned, but left without saying another word.

The next day, Vuse called for an urgent meeting of the transformation committee. They would meet at lunch time in Bill's office. He demanded that everyone attend the meeting. He would not accept any excuses whatsoever. When asked what the meeting was about, he simply said. "I have something to say. Make sure you're there on time."

Vuse looked at the listless group, slouching in their chairs. He stood up and spoke firmly. "I don't know what is happening to our transformation committee, but this cannot continue any longer," he declared. "We were elected by our people with a mandate to transform this factory. We have a responsibility to perform our mandate. But look at us now. Everyone is walking around depressed, tired and sick. No one wants to attend meetings any more. We've given up. We've lost our spirit. And we're the so called leaders of the transformation in this company! What do you think our people think of us?"

His voice softened: "I know we're all hurting. I know the last meeting brought up some painful memories for us. But if we don't get past this and begin transforming ourselves and our factory, we'll be letting down our people. And we'll be letting ourselves down." He paused and stared at each person in turn; "What I want to know is this: are we really committed to transformation? Are we prepared to go through some discomfort to achieve our goals? Like our heroes, are we prepared to face a personal struggle? Or are we simply going to give up when the going gets tough?"

The room was quiet. It was as though each person was struggling to make sense of the emotions battling for control inside him. Finally Sipho spoke. "I really did have to finish some work last week. I wasn't shirking." He smiled broadly. "You couldn't manage the transformation without me. I'm in."

Rosalie spoke hesitantly: "I don't know what has been happening to me this last week. I know I should be feeling so excited. Mr Price liked my designs. Bill has asked me to do more. It's what I've wanted for a long time. But I just seem to have lost all my energy. I really am committed to our transformation. But it seems quite difficult right now."

Bill cleared his throat; "I'm also feeling quite down right now, but I'm still committed to the transformation."

"So am I," said each group member in turn.

Vuse smiled sympathetically. "So it's agreed we will continue the transformation process – even though it's a bit tough right now?" They all nodded. "OK, we'll have our next meeting at 3.30 p.m. on Friday – no excuses accepted." They all smiled. As they left the office, each person in turn shook Vuse's hand.

Bill looked gratefully at Vuse. "Thanks for calling this meeting. I should have responded far earlier to this crisis. I don't know what has happened to me lately, but I've lost all my energy for things. I know that is unacceptable from a leader. I'm sorry to have let you down."

"It's all right." Vuse's tone was calm and reassuring. "But you and I have some homework to do before that meeting. On Friday we are going to have to turn around the energy of the group. I'm not sure how we're going to do it. Have you found any more of your American sangoma cards lately?"

Bill shook his head. "It's a pity – we sure could use some help on this."

'When I really need a tiger card, there's none to be found,' Bill thought wryly. He'd searched through his in-tray, hoping for a miracle. There was nothing. He'd walked slowly to his car, desperately scanning the littered pavements for a flash of purple. There was nothing. On a whim, he'd taken a detour on the way home, and walked around the only park in Sandton. But he'd found nothing. No tiger cards. No inspiration. Nothing at all. He sat down beside the pond and watched the ducks drifting aimlessly.

"That's what I'm doing right now," he thought. "I'm floating around in a sea of depression. I haven't been providing any direction to my team. I haven't been leading by example. If it hadn't been for Vuse we'd all be sinking right now. Where am I going to find another tiger card? I can't handle the next meeting alone. I need some help..."

Bill's thoughts were interrupted by a shout. He looked around. A father was kicking a soccer ball to his five-year-old son. The ball had landed in a rose garden. The boy was holding the ball to his ear. Then he held the ball to his face. Then back to his ear. "I think it has a hole in it," he shouted. "Don't worry," his dad said calmly, "we'll fix it at home."

Bill walked slowly to his car, thinking about the father's reassuring words: "Don't worry, we'll fix it at home". He thought of his home. America, Sharon, Brad, Rose.

Rose. A surge of excitement pulsated through his body. He remembered how Rose had explained things so clearly to him the last time he'd felt confused and depressed. She'd know what to do. He had to get hold of her immediately.

He felt a twinge of disappointment on hearing her answering machine. "Hi Rose, its Bill calling from South Africa. I think I'm in more than the usual chaos right now and would really appreciate your wisdom. It is urgent in that I'm meeting with my transformation team on Friday. I need to know what to do before then. I'll email you..."

Her answering machine beeped. He had run out of time. He put the phone down and booted up his computer. He began writing. It was 1 O'clock when he felt his shoulders throbbing. He looked at the 12 pages he had written. He hoped that Rose would read it in time. He pressed 'Send' and went to bed. For the first time in weeks he felt a spark of hope dancing in his mind. He slept deeply.

On awakening he immediately put on his computer. He heard it booting up while he showered. He found himself humming. As he brushed his teeth, he went into his email. "Yes!" he shouted with glee, spitting out his toothpaste onto his keyboard. "There she is." He threw his toothbrush aside and eagerly read Rose's response. He sat thoughtfully for a while, and then he smiled. He knew what he had to do. He looked at his watch. He was late. He pressed 'Print', bent down to collect his toothbrush, and went back to the bathroom.

Vuse read Rose's email thoughtfully. "There never is an easy solution, is there?" he commented.

"I think we should share it with the transformation team and maybe try out some of her exercises," suggested Bill.

"Hmm," agreed Vuse. "But this is deep stuff. Each person must be allowed to decide for themselves how far they want to go."

The meeting started at 3.30 p.m. Everyone arrived on time, keen to show their commitment to the process. Bill began by reading Rose's letter.

Dear Bill,

You are right. This is not the usual 'chaos' stage that you were experiencing before. It is something far deeper and far more painful. It is possible to do something to 'turn the energy of the group around'. But this is not something that can be done in a single meeting. It is going to require some effort, and a great deal of courage from each member of your team. Let me explain.

When we experience a traumatic event in our lives, both our bod-

ies and our souls are affected. While our physical wounds usually get treated immediately, our emotional pain is often ignored. Once our bodies have healed, we are expected to 'get back to normal'. We try to, but can't understand why we keep getting overwhelmed by feelings of fear, rage, or sorrow. We feel we want to run away, lash out or sob. But we can't. We know that losing control of our emotions is not socially acceptable. We're told that we need to 'put it all behind us' and 'get on with our lives.' So we do. We learn to cope by focusing our attention externally. We brush aside our feelings and put all our energy into our jobs, our children, or our causes. We create a new socially acceptable persona for ourselves. Once in a while an inexplicable emotion overwhelms us. A feeling of pain, bitterness, anger, or disappointment bubbles to the surface – a faint echo of an event buried deep in our memories. We feel surprised, or even embarrassed by the emotion. We quickly bury it under an avalanche of activity.

Some of us live out our personas until the day we die. Some of us are forced to confront our true selves when our adopted roles are no longer needed – our children have left home, we've retired or the cause we've dedicated our lives to has been lost or won.

Some of us face a single moment in which our masks are stripped aside to reveal our raw, authentic selves. Perhaps we've suddenly found ourselves surrounded by a particularly caring group of people. Someone opens up and reveals a vulnerability. The group responds with love and acceptance. We lower our guard for a moment, and our true self bubbles out. We feel a moment of relief as our façade falls away, and we reveal the festering emotional boil that we have been ashamed to let others see. As others uncover their blisters and boils, we realise we are not alone.

Once the moment has passed, we often feel uncomfortable about having revealed so much of our true self to others. What if our colleagues don't like the Self we've just revealed? What if they pity or avoid us? We have been comfortable in the role we've been living. We are not sure we want to revert back to our authentic selves again. So we put on our masks again and pretend nothing happened.

Having shared a very special moment with each other, each of you now have a difficult choice to make. You can retreat into your trusted persona and pretend the moment didn't happen. Or you can use the moment to begin a process of personal transformation. The choice is yours to make as individuals. The easiest and safest option is to carry on as normal. And that is a perfectly acceptable choice to make. Personal transformation can be a long and difficult journey to undertake.

For those of you who do undertake the journey to transformation, you will need to pass through three places before you reach your destination, namely the cities of revealing, healing, and self discovery. Revealing is a messy and painful process akin to lancing a boil. Anger, hatred, and bitterness have to be released before you can begin to heal your wounded psyche. Healing involves accepting and nurturing your shy, wounded Self. As you begin to feel better about yourself, you will begin to discover what your special life purpose is. You will then feel more alive, more positive, and more fulfilled than you have ever felt before.

So what do I recommend to your team?

1) Each team member must decide whether he or she is prepared to 'confront their demons' in order to achieve personal growth and meaning. As this can be a painful process, it must be a personal decision – not a team decision.

2) The team needs to provide a safe and caring environment for those that go through the exercises and for those who choose not to.

At this stage you may be asking yourselves "How do we go about stripping away our masks and finding our Selves?" The answer is difficult. There is no one right single way. In America, many people rely on psychologists. However, should you prefer to work independently, you could use a very powerful approach called 'journal therapy.' It works like this. Each individual works alone in the following way:

1) Get an A4 pad of paper.

2) Each morning, upon wakening write three pages. You can write anything that comes to mind. It may be household chores that need to be done. It may be how you're feeling. It may be something that is bothering you. Write anything at all – no matter how trivial it seems to you. But make sure you complete three pages each day before you go to work.

3) Try not to look back at what you've written, or to attempt to analyse or correct your work. Simply keep writing.

Initially you will find it difficult to write. You'll wonder how you're going to fill three pages. You won't know what to write about. Don't let that put you off. Keep writing. Remember, you are trying to re-establish a relationship with your real Self. Your long lost friend with whom you've lost contact. It will take time to get reacquainted.

After a few weeks you'll notice something amazing happening. As you begin to write, you will slip into a type of reverie. Your fears, anger, hopes and dreams will begin to flow through your pen. It is as though you are writing a letter to a trusted friend –your best friend. Someone who understands you and all you've been through. Your Self. And then, one day, your Self will appear in your writing. Answers to impossible dilemmas will materialise on your page. Insights will emerge explaining why you feel the way you do, and why others are behaving the way they are. After about three weeks, you may like to read back though your journal and underline any insights you've gained, and actions you feel you need to take.

A few important points to remember about process:

1) Each person is responsible for their own healing. However, it is critical that each of you feels that you are surrounded by a group of friends who care about you, and what you may be feeling. This will keep you grounded in the present, as you explore your past.

2) As a team, you may want to discuss how you can encourage and support one another as you write your personal journals. After about a few weeks, you may wish to share your insights and chosen actions with the team with the understanding that the team will try to help you to accomplish whatever you feel you need to do.

This should provide you with a useful starting point, Bill. I have a few more exercises you could look at later. Good luck with what you are embarking upon.

With love

Rose

PS Please tell your team they sound like very special people indeed.

PPS. I am going to the Middle East to do some consulting. I will contact you as soon as I get back."

"And that's the end of the email," concluded Bill. "What do you think of what you've just heard?"

The group was silent for a while.

Then Jay spoke up.

"I don't feel very comfortable with all this getting in touch with your feelings stuff!"

Koos nodded in agreement.

Jay continued: "Anyway, it's too American."

Sipho stood up. "I agree with Jay. We need African solutions for African problems."

Bill felt disappointed by their response. He'd been so excited by Rose's email. He'd really expected the group to respond more positively.

The preacher in Sipho demanded to be heard: "We are a transformation committee. We have a mandate to our people. We must conform to our original mandate."

"Oh No!" thought Bill, "here we go again." He caught Vuse's eye.

Vuse immediately interrupted Sipho's flow: "And how would you define that mandate, Sipho?"

Sipho was impatient. "We've been through this a thousand times already. It's about getting training, and overtime for our people."

"Yes that's true. But is that all?" questioned Vuse.

"No! we want better wages too."

Vuse was silent.

"And maternity leave," added Sipho in frustration.

Vuse looked around the room. "Then it's simple. All we need to do is to ask Bill here for a wage increase, overtime and training and we can disband our committee. Bill can return to America. Our factory will be shipped to Malaysia, and we will all have achieved our purpose. Is that our mandate as leaders?"

"Every time we speak about our mandate it changes. Why can't we just agree on our mandate and stick to it?" Jay demanded in frustration.

Doris rose. "We forget things too quickly. Do you remember the meeting we had where we all spoke about people who had meant a lot to us in our lives. I spoke about my mother, a warm and caring woman, who was always there to listen to me. You said you wanted to be like your father, Vuse. You wanted to help people in our factory believe they could do and become anything. And you Nandi, wanted to be like your brother. Strong and full of courage. Sipho, you spoke about your sister. You were going to help people feel proud of who they are. And you Mr Bill. You spoke about your grandmother. You wanted to help people to learn and to grow."

"I still do," Bill said wistfully. "What excited me so much about that particular meeting is that for the first time I believed that I was part of a special team of people. Together we were going to do far more than simply save the factory. We were going to make the South African Branded Apparel factory the best factory in the world. I pictured our team creating a factory full of purpose and meaning. A place where everyone could become their personal best. I could see business men from around the world visiting our factory to learn from us how to run a successful factory."

Rosalie sighed. "I also felt so positive during that meeting. I was going to be just like my fourth grade teacher. I was going to encourage my staff to believe in themselves and in their dreams. But right now, I'm feeling so depressed, I'm not sure I can motivate myself, let alone inspire anyone else."

"So let's summarise what we've just discussed." Vuse took the lead again. "We as leaders have a purpose to fulfil. One that is far greater than simply fighting for more pay, or overtime. We want to inspire our people to live out what is great and wonderful within them. Now Rosalie raises an interesting point about leadership. Where does leadership start? Do we start with others, or with ourselves? Can we inspire others if we are feeling depressed? Can we make others feel special if we are feeling out of sorts? Can we lead others if we have no direction or purpose in our own lives?"

Sipho looked thoughtful. "Nelson Mandela is one of the greatest leaders in the world. While he was in jail, he spent a lot of time in self contemplation. If he had the will to do this for 27 years, surely we can try out these exercises for six weeks?"

Bill looked at the group. They were all nodding in agreement.

Doris remained concerned. "What if I'm no good at writing? Can I write in Xhosa?" she asked. "Can I write in Afrikaans then?" demanded Koos. Bill felt relieved. These were objections he could deal with. "You can write in any language you feel comfortable with," he assured them.

Koos spoke hesitantly. "What if I don't want to bring up all that stuff about the war again?"

Bill responded gently. "You have a very valid concern Koos. All I can say is that I've done a similar exercise to this before. The one thing to remember is that no one but you is going to see what you write about. You can write about anything you choose. And you don't have to write about anything that you don't want to. Whatever you choose to do, is the right thing for you."

"That's right," Vuse added "Whatever each of you decide to do, is OK with all of us."

Bill pointed to the pile of A4 notepads on his desk. "There is a notepad, a pen and a copy of Rose's email for each of you that wants to take part in this exercise. Please help yourselves on your way out."

They joked with one another as they left clutching their notepads and pens. "Sipho, it's three pages of normal size writing – not one word per line," Nandi called out.

"When I sell my autobiography and I'm famous, you'll be lining up for my autograph," he retorted.

"What's it going to be called?" Jay shouted. "The long walk to the factory?" They'd laughed, their bravado masking the hope and fear they were all feeling.

It was as Rose had predicted. The team found it difficult to fill the three pages at first. Then, as they became used to writing every day, they were surprised by what emerged from their writing.

"I couldn't believe how angry I was," Nandi confessed at a meeting weeks later. "I was angry with the apartheid government who had murdered my brother in cold blood. I was angry with the white people for allowing it to happen. I was angry with my parents who didn't do anything to prevent it happening. I was angry with myself for being so helpless. I was so angry it scared me. But then I suddenly realised I was just a child at the time. I shouldn't blame myself for something the apartheid government had done."

"Of course not," Bill responded softly.

"I was also surprised by my anger," admitted Bill. "I was angry at Sharon and Brad for leaving me. I was angry with my previous company for treating me so badly when they fired me. I was angry with Jannie for deceiving me when I arrived here. I was angry at the people who mugged me outside the factory. I was angry with the crime and violence of this country. But then I realised that most of all, I was angry at myself. I had given up control of my life to others. I had allowed others to determine how I felt."

The words tumbled out of Koos: "Now I understand why I have trouble sleeping at night. I didn't know that I was keeping so much anger inside of me. I was angry with the government for the lies they had told us. We were led to believe that we were fighting a war of survival. A war against evil. Against communism. Then the government sold us down the river. What reward do I get for serving my country? 'Affirmative Action.' I'm lucky to even have a job now at all as a white. And my friends who gave up their lives in the war – it was all for nothing. From now on, I'm not going to follow other's orders. I'm going to do what I think is right."

"I'm so relieved all of you felt the same way. I was getting worried about how full of rage I was". The group looked surprised at Rosalie's loud and confident tone. "I was furious with my parents. Why didn't they care that Piet was beating me? Why didn't they help me? I found myself becoming especially angry with my mother. Why didn't she leave my father when he abused her? But most of all I was angry with myself. Why did I put up with Piet for so long?" Her voice softened. "Then I realised I had been too hard on myself and on my mother. We each did what we could do at the time."

"It was hard for me to admit to myself, but I was angry with my sister." Sipho confessed. "I had always resented my sister for being the favourite one in the family. She was the clever one. She had the good job. She got all the attention. Then she got Aids, and suddenly I had to take care of her. I found myself feeling angry with her for not protecting herself. I was angry with her for forcing me to lie to our parents. I was angry that I had to put my own life on hold because she was sick... And yet I couldn't admit this to anyone. They would have thought I was selfish. As I wrote, I realised that I'd been jealous of my sister. I didn't believe I was as good as her. Then I realised

I have many strengths too..."

"I thought I'd come to terms with my father's death, but I hadn't," conceded Jay. "I must have filled up about seven pages describing what I'd do to the people who murdered my father, if ever I caught up with them. But then I found myself being angry with my father. He'd known that they wanted to kill him; why hadn't he taken precautions? And I was angry at myself – for not doing more to protect my father. Even though I was only 12 at the time."

"But you couldn't have done anything. You were only a child!" exclaimed Nandi.

"I know that now," said Jay.

Vuse spoke up next: "You called me a hero, but I'm not. I too found myself becoming angry at my life. I was angry at my parents for being so poor – for making me have to struggle for everything. I was angry at the university for the disdainful way they treated me. I was angry with Jannie, for his mocking attitude towards blacks. I was angry with the whites who had all the wealth in the country, and left us the crumbs."

"But you've got so much to be proud about!" exclaimed Sipho. "You've achieved so much. You're our role model."

"I know," grinned Vuse. "Sometimes it's hard to accept yourself as you are, rather than as you were..."

Doris began speaking. "I was also very angry. I was angry at the apartheid government for what they did to me. I was also angry at myself for not defending myself more. I was angry at the white people for not caring about what was happening to us. And I was angry at you too, Mr Bill, for coming from America, where everything is so easy." She paused and smiled at Bill.

"But then after all my anger came out, I found myself thinking about the good side of my life. I remembered my mother and what she'd taught me about being a good person. I thought of what I had that I could share with our people. I thought of all the things you, Mr Bill, have done for us. You know, you are the first white person to care about us. I want to say thank you for all you are doing. We know we haven't been easy..."

The tears welled up in Bill's eyes.

Vuse interrupted the moment: "Thank you Doris. You are saying what we have all wanted to say for a long time. Bill and I have spent many evenings together discussing ways we could help the people at Branded Apparel. To me, he has become far more than a boss. He has become like a father."

The group applauded. Vuse held up his hand. "But there is something else I want to share with you about our leader." Bill looked apprehensive. "Our leader is not working alone. He is being guided by some very powerful spirits." The group looked intrigued. Vuse continued. "Bill, I wonder if you can show us one of your American sangoma cards?" Vuse passed the purple card around. "Bill has an American sangoma. Whenever he needs advice on something important, a card like this finds its way to him." Each member of the group inspected the card.

"See the words, *Polish away the grime to reveal the shine*?". They nodded. "We've been doing just that these last three weeks. Every day, with every page we've written, we've polished away the grime of our past. It has been difficult. It's been messy. But now that we've polished away our anger, our ubuntu has begun to shine through. That is how it should be."

"I have just thought of something," Doris exclaimed. "This is what we've been talking about all this time. This is the type of factory we should be creating. One filled with ubuntu."

"An African factory for the people of Africa," echoed Sipho.

The words blurted out of Rosalie: "I had an insight while I was writing. I really feel good when I am designing. Why can't we design a unique range of clothing for Branded Apparel? It could have an African theme?"

"And," added Jay, "We could buy South African materials. We could support job creation in our country by only buying local."

"We could also train unemployed women to sew. Then when we're too busy, they can help us," suggested Doris.

Nandi was looking around the factory. "This factory has been irritating me for ages. If we moved some of the work stations around, we could do things much quicker around here." Nandi was already on her feet. "Sipho, come here and help me move this some tables..."

Before long, Nandi had the whole team spring cleaning

the factory. Off-cuts were given away to the homeless, the litter outside the factory was removed and the workstations were rearranged making the factory feel more spacious. One Monday morning, Bill arrived to find the walls painted a cheerful yellow.

"Now this is a place where ubuntu can flourish," declared Nandi with satisfaction.

The spirit of transformation was reflected in their work too. Bill and Vuse had laughed as Bill recounted the words of the buyer from Edgars: "There has been an amazing turnaround in your lines. What quality system did you put into your factory?"

"It gave me great satisfaction to be able to say 'none at all'. I don't believe in quality systems. I believe in quality people!" explained Bill.

The rush of positive energy lasted three weeks. Then suddenly, a cloud of lethargy enveloped Branded Apparel.

Bill sought out Vuse. "What is going on? I thought we'd made a breakthrough. Everyone was so motivated, and so full of energy. And now, it is as if the spirit has been sucked out of the factory all over again."

Bill noticed the lines that had suddenly appeared around Vuse's eyes."I don't understand it myself. I spoke to everyone and no one can explain it." Vuse shrugged his shoulders. "I think we've gone back to where we started." A wave of panic surged through Bill. Vuse was the one that had kept them going. If Vuse had given up then they were in trouble.

That night, he tried to phone Rose, but she was still in Saudi Arabia. He tried Sharon, but he only got through to her answering machine. He searched through his database of contacts, until he found Louise. She was a qualified psychologist who'd been on his MBA programme. She would know what to do. He dialed her number. She was delighted to hear from him. Of course she'd help him. He spoke. A torrent of words poured out of his soul, sweeping away his loneliness.

Finally he concluded: "What do I do now?"

Louise's reaction crushed him. She was angry: "I can't believe what you've just told me. You've made a mess of people's lives and now you expect me to fix it up in a single phone call. You've opened up things that you can't even begin to deal with. What made you think that you could read a few books, try out a few exercises and that's all there is to psychotherapy? Who is this woman, Rose, who told you to do 'journal therapy?' I should report her to the psychology board. Journal therapy of all things. These people have been through real trauma. They need properly trained psychologists – not some exercises handed out over an email by a pop psychologist. I don't think you realise it. You say you care about these people; well, you could have done these people some serious damage..."

7 A Flash of Gold and Black in the Night

The most potent muse of all is your inner child

— Stephen Nachmanovitch

Bill tore open the DHL courier bag that had arrived unexpectedly from Abu Dhabi. Inside the envelope he found nothing but an Arab Emirates paper napkin with some words scrawled on it. Somebody had obviously written this note in haste. His eyes scanned the writing until he found the signature. It was from Rose. He returned to the beginning of the message and read eagerly.

"You'll never guess what – I found one of your special cards in the most unlikely place. I was at Dubai airport checking in for my flight to Abu Dhabi. Suddenly this dark-eyed man bashes into me. He grabs me, twirls me around and apologises. Then he's off again. Next thing I see three men dressed in long Arabian robes and red and white checked headscarves running towards me. They want to know if he gave me anything. I shake my head. They look at me intently. Then they run after him. On the plane I discover one of your special cards in my pocket.

I don't know if this is what they were after, but I felt I had to courier the card to you immediately. What is the secret of these cards?"

Bill shook the serviette. Nothing fell out. His heart pounded as he rummaged through the wastepaper bin searching for the envelope he'd just discarded. He found it and felt inside. There was something sharp in the bottom corner. He pulled it out and read its message aloud.

satisfy the inner child first

He read the words again, and again, wondering what they meant. A minute later he jumped from his chair and raced out of the door.

"Vuse… he's back. Our American sangoma is back!" Bill cried out.

Vuse put down his clipboard and hurried into Bill's office. The rest of the team followed him in. "What does it say? let's see it!" they demanded.

satisfy the inner child first

"What does it mean?"

"I don't know," responded Bill. "It is something we are going to have to interpret for ourselves. That is how these sangoma cards work."

"Maybe the child refers to our selves?" mused Vuse.

"How do we go about satisfying it?" Koos mumbled.

Sipho shook his head. "This is quite a riddle. How long

do we have to solve it?"

Bill laughed. "No time at all and all of our lives. I'm beginning to understand that we have to master what each card says before we get the next American sangoma card."

"sangoma," Vuse murmured to himself. "That's who can help us interpret this card."

He stood up. "I'm going out to see our African sangoma now, if that's alright with you Bill."

Bill grabbed his jacket; "Good idea. While you do that, I'm going to visit a bookstore. Maybe I'll find an idea there that can help us."

"Can I come with you?" asked Nandi.

"Me too," demanded Rosalie.

"Well then I'm going to see some friends of my own," insisted Sipho.

"I'll come with you," said Jay

Doris and Koos offered to stay behind to manage the factory.

As they raced down the stairs, Nandi let out a shriek of delight: "I feel just like a naughty kid again. It's like we're bunking school."

"Yes, it's fun, isn't it?" agreed Bill.

"I haven't done anything like this since I started working," admitted Vuse.

"The first one to solve the riddle gets a free jacket designed by our own world famous designer, Rosalie," Sipho shouted as they went off in different directions.

Vuse was the last to return to the factory. The group

was waiting impatiently for him.

"What took you so long?" demanded Nandi.

"Yeah, you've lost out. I've already won the jacket," Sipho teased.

"Forget it," insisted Nandi. "We have the answer, and we got back first."

"OK, OK," laughed Bill. "Let's hear what everyone has to say first. Then Koos and Doris will decide who gets the jacket. Vuse we'll start with you."

A pensive Vuse spoke softly. "I had a very strange experience. As you know, no one books an appointment to see a sangoma. You just go there. Yet, when I entered the dark hut, she said in a strong clear voice: 'I've been expecting you', as if she knew I was coming to see her. She instructed me to sit down. I sat silently, waiting for her speak. But she shut her eyes and seemed to be in a trance. Suddenly she spoke in a voice that wasn't her own. It was a child's voice and it said: 'The child is crying. It is time to stop crying. Let the child play.'

She then began to shudder in an awful way as though a spirit was leaving her body. Suddenly she was quiet. She collapsed on the floor. I wanted to ask her to explain what she meant – but she told me to leave. When I got to the car I realised that I hadn't even told her why I'd come to see her. She didn't even know about our card."

"Aha!" summarised Koos. "So we must satisfy our child by playing."

"Wow!" exclaimed Bill. "This is simply awesome! Nandi show them what we found."

Nandi held up a colourful book. It looked like it had been put together by a child who had just been given a set of 24 coloured pens. It was covered in stars, circles, drawings and childish writing.

"Let me read you something from the Inspiration Sandwhich by SARK. It's just like what Vuse's sangoma said."

Remember the sandbox?
All you needed was bare toes in warm sand,
and maybe a good bucket.
Then you could build your world.
We all have wonderful new worlds to build.

"Hmm; so by playing we can build a wonderful world," Koos murmured.

"Hold on," interrupted Sipho. "What I've got to show you definitely wins the prize." He held up a set of brightly coloured playing cards. On the front of each card was a picture of a child trailing a blanket behind him. On the back was some writing. "I remembered seeing these at a friend of mine's. His wife is very into this sort of thing. It was written by Sandy Goldberg. Let me read them to you. And then Rosalie, I'll tell you how I want you to design my jacket."

Take a child by the hand & follow where it leads you.
Children are enthusiastic about simple things.
Children love unconditionally.

Children's imaginations are not restricted.
Children let their spirits guide them.
Children see only possibilities
Children persevere until they get it right.
Children trust.
Children have fun.

"That's exactly what ubuntu is all about!" declared Doris. It is about being like you were when you were a child. Before you got hurt by life."

The group was silent as they reflected on her words.

Bill suddenly cried out: "I feel as though I've just awoken from a deep sleep. For years, I've been trying to mould myself on others. I've read text books. I've listened to consultants. I've been on training courses. Only now do I understand the truth. We all simply need to be as we really are. As we were born to be."

"We were all born with abundant love. Then the system took it away from us. That was the real tragedy of apartheid," mused Vuse. "The sangoma said it is time for the child to stop crying and to start playing. We as leaders need to stop crying about how we've been hurt in the past, and recapture the playful spirit of the child in our hearts and in our factory."

"But there is a good reason why we lost our inner child," insisted Jay. "We had to in order to survive."

"That's true," Nandi concurred. "What happens if we become full of caring and the people around us don't? Won't we be taken advantage of?"

Vuse spoke softly. "What you're asking is, can we be full of caring in a world without compassion? Can we be filled with love and trust in a world of cynical adults?"

"What are we all so afraid of?" Doris blurted out in frustration. "After all we've been through, are we now scared of losing our unhappiness? I sometimes think we would rather be hurt by being who we're not, than risk being happy by being who we really are. The sangoma said it's time to stop crying. It is time to listen to her. It is time to listen to our Selves!"

Koos coughed. "I'm sorry to interrupt. I know I haven't seen a sangoma or anything, but I have something I'd like to share with you. You know, while I was writing my three pages everyday, I was worried about how much anger and hatred I had inside me. I then began wondering how Nelson Mandela had managed to stay so full of love while he was in jail. So I decided to buy his book to find out how to deal with my own hatred. There is a wonderful quote in his book *Long Walk to Freedom* that I need to share with you. It helped me so much."

He began reading confidently:

Our deepest fear is not that we are inadequate.
Our deepest fear is that
we are powerful beyond measure.
It is our light, not our darkness,
that most frightens us.
We ask ourselves, who am I to be brilliant, gorgeous,
talented, and fabulous?

Actually, who are you not to be?
You are a child of God.
Your playing small doesn't serve the world.
There is nothing enlightened about shrinking
so that other people don't feel insecure around you.
We are born to make manifest the Glory of God that is within us.
It's not just in some of us, it's in everyone,
and as we let our own light shine,
we unconsciously give other people permission to do the same.
As we are liberated from our own fear,
our presence automatically liberates others.

"That is what Nelson Mandela wrote," he concluded. "If after all he'd been through in jail, he has the courage to shine, I'm going to try to do the same."

Doris enveloped Koos in a bear hug. "You are a very special person you know," she said warmly. He grinned sheepishly.

"Its really nice to work here," commented Mary, the new recruit, a month later. "There is a really special feel about Branded Apparel!"

Bill looked around the factory with pride. He could barely recognise the place. People were sewing and packing to the beat of Kwaito music. Above the music, Bill could hear Doris mothering Koos, and Nandi teasing Jay. Sipho had built a special yellow wheelbarrow which he was using to move shirts from one end of the factory to the other. Bill's eyes were drawn to the posters decorating the walls of the factory. They were full of inspirational quotations that had been brought in by staff members. He'd never seen them so full of energy before.

Bill reflected on what his team had managed to achieve during the last month. Production was at an all-time high. Customers who had once threatened never to do business with Branded Apparel again, were now giving them repeat orders. The numbers were beginning to look very impressive indeed. They had turned the factory around.

But Bill was aware that the challenge was not yet over. There was still the threat of Malaysia hanging over them. To keep the factory in South Africa they needed to be more than successful. They needed to prove they were the best in the world. It was time to begin creating his centre of excellence.

At their next meeting, he put the challenge to the team.

"We've created a special factory, filled with ubuntu. Our staff and our customers are happy. We can rightly feel proud of ourselves. But this means little to head office. They still see us as one tiny factory in Africa, competing with hundreds of factories around the world. It is time for us to show the world what we in Africa can do. It is time for us to shine our special light on the world.

"Another riddle," observed Sipho. "I don't suppose you have an answer to this one either?"

Bill shook his head. "All I know is we shouldn't wait for America to tell us what to do. I believe that with a bit of creativity, we could come up with something that makes us special. Something that the rest of the world wants to get from our factory in South Africa."

"An African solution to the world's problems. I like that!" laughed Jay.

"Any ideas on where to begin?" asked Bill.

"I have an idea," Rosalie spoke shyly. Sipho was about to tease her when Vuse put up his hand to stop him.

"When I was a child I used to love painting. I was quite good in fact. But I gave it up after a teacher laughed at one of my pictures. While writing my three pages, I discovered I wanted to paint again. But I didn't know where to start. I found a book that teaches you how to rediscover your inner creativity. There is a technique in the book that our team could try out. It works like this. Each week we should treat ourselves by going on an outing together – somewhere outside of the factory. You see, when we're out of our usual surroundings, we expose our subconscious selves to different sights, sounds, tastes, smells and textures. That is when our creativity begins to flow."

"That's what happened when I went to see the sangoma, and you went to a bookstore," exclaimed Vuse.

"You mean to say that bunking can be good for us?" giggled Nandi.

"Limited bunking," admonished Doris. "We still have a factory to run."

"Why don't we try it out and see what happens. Who wants to suggest a place for our first team treat?" asked Bill.

"I know where we can go this week!" exclaimed Sipho.

"Bafana Bafana is playing Cameroon on Saturday. I can get tickets to the match."

"What has soccer got to do with Branded Apparel?" asked Doris.

"That's the whole point. You have to discover the connection yourself," retorted Sipho, looking to Rosalie for confirmation.

"Anyway," he continued quickly, "I expect you all to arrive wearing Bafana Bafana colours. We'll meet here at my house at noon."

"Have you ever been in a black taxi before Bill?" asked Doris. He shook his head as they laughed. "Well you're in for quite an experience!"

The battered blue combi was already rocking as Bill mounted the step. Sipho steered him past the toyi toying dancers to the back of the van. Nandi immediately joined the dancers. The rest of the team followed Bill.

A gold and black shirted youth waved his beer at Bill. "Who is going to win today?" he shouted.

"Bafana Bafana of course," responded Bill cautiously.

"That's right my broer. Bafana Bafana," he sang.

"Bafana Bafana," the supporters sang in chorus. Sipho guided Bill to an empty seat, as the taxi sped off. Another taxi raced past them, hooting its horn. Hanging out of the windows were South African supporters waving flags, beers and caps.

About a kilometer from the stadium, the combi stopped. The road ahead was blocked by hundreds of taxis. Many had stopped in the middle of the road to unload their passengers. Other taxis had tried to overtake them on the left and on the right, causing the traffic to stop completely. Complicating the situation were those taxis trying to turn their vehicles around whilst others tried to pass them. Bill could barely hear Sipho above the hooting of the frustrated drivers. Sipho signalled Bill to follow him.

"Try not to get lost," cautioned Sipho. "Otherwise we'll never be able to find one another in this crowd."

"How many people are here?" asked Bill.

"The stadium can hold 80,000 people. I guess there must be 100,000 here today. Luckily we have tickets," answered Sipho.

"This is like a carnival," exclaimed Bill. "Look at those people with their faces painted. It looks like such fun."

Rosalie pointed to a sign saying 'Faces painted R10'.

"Why don't you get your face done?" she dared.

"I will if you will," he responded recklessly.

"OK," said Rosalie defiantly. "We both want our faces painted, and he's paying," she said to the teenager standing next to the sign.

Rosalie sat on the green plastic chair at the side of the road. The street artist began painting a big green 'Y' across Rosalie's forehead and down her nose. The top of the 'Y' was filled in by a small yellow 'V' and a black 'V' inside of that. One of Rosalie's cheeks was painted red, and the other blue.

"What is he painting?" asked Bill.

"The South African flag," responded Doris proudly.

"OK, your turn now," taunted Rosalie. The artist looked at Bill with amusement.

"Sit here," he ordered. The sticky paint tickled Bill's cheeks. He tried to keep still while the rest of the team laughed at him. A few minutes later it was all over.

"Now you look like a umuntu," commented the artist. "You just need a T-shirt to match your face." Jay signalled to a hawker at the opposite side of the road. The eager woman scurried towards them. "How many?" she asked.

"Just one T-shirt for him," instructed Jay. "And seven beers for us."

As they entered the stadium, Bill looked at the 100,000 supporters dancing in the stands. Everyone was dressed in either Bafana Bafana or South African colours.

Jay read his thoughts. "Just imagine if Branded Apparel was the company manufacturing all these T-shirts," he commented.

A group of supporters in the stand next door to them had stood up and raised their hands. The next group did the same. A Mexican wave spread swiftly across the stadium. It was their turn to stand up. "We'd have a potential market of at least 100,000," responded Bill as he sat down again. The Mexican wave continued on its path.

Bill turned towards Rosalie. "What if..." he began. The stadium erupted. Shouts of "La Duuuuma" filled the air. A group of women behind them began ululating. Bafana Bafana had scored a goal. Bill felt himself being embraced by a fat woman standing above him in the stands. One hundred thousand people were laughing, crying, dancing and shouting.

"I couldn't hear you. What did you say?" asked Rosalie, as the crowd sat down again.

"Imagine if we could capture this energy and this spirit in our clothes," mused Bill.

"That would be quite a challenge" she responded thoughtfully.

"So what did you think of the soccer match, Bill?" asked Sipho as they drove home.

"It was an incredible experience Sipho, thank you for organising it."

"So," Sipho asked Doris triumphantly,"What does soccer have to do with Branded Apparel?"

"Everyone was wearing clothes that hadn't been made by Branded Apparel!" retorted Doris.

"But imagine if we could change that." Sipho shouted in excitement. " We could sponsor the team's clothes. Imagine if the Bafana Bafana team were seen wearing our clothes."

"And imagine if all the fans were kitted out in our clothes too," added Nandi.

"There must have been 100,000 supporters here today. That's an enormous market."

The ever-serious Jay burst out. "That's nothing. At the African Nations Cup, they play to full stadiums every day for weeks."

"And what about the World Cup?" Sipho could barely contain his excitement. "Imagine if we got the World Cup Tournament in South Africa in 2006, and we were the official suppliers of T-shirts..."

Bill was convinced. "This idea has a lot of potential Sipho. But we need to research it further. Jay, can you find out who is currently making the T-shirt that I'm wearing. Are they the only suppliers? Did they have to get permission to sell these shirts at the stadium? Sipho, can you find out how many soccer matches are planned for this year? Is there a fan club for Bafana Bafana? How many members does it have? How could we get access to these members?"

Sipho's face broke into a grin. "My brother-in-law is an assistant coach for Bafana Bafana. I'll go see him this evening."

"Hold on," interrupted Nandi. " I hope this doesn't mean that our treats are over. I was just getting to enjoy myself. Bill, it's your turn next week. Take us somewhere American. We want to see what the rest of the world is doing."

"OK, OK," Bill pretended to sigh. "We'll continue the outings for a month, and see what ideas come out. Then we must begin working on our centre of excellence - before its too late."

All that week, Bill agonised over where he could take his team. Where in South Africa could he show them America? How could he show them what was happening in the world, without travelling?

It was Brad who supplied the obvious answer.

"Hey dad," the email read. "Check out my new website at brad@geocities.cam. PS. How is life in Africa?"

Bill grinned. "When you want answers, ask your children," he thought.

"Where are you taking us?" complained Sipho. "This looks like a shop."

"We're going to meet my son Brad," Bill said mysteriously with a grin on his face.

Doris looked at the rows of brightly coloured boxes adorning the shelves of the store.

"Does he work here?" asked Doris. "I thought he was in America."

"He is," Bill grinned. "That's where we're going today."

"Another riddle," mumbled Sipho as Bill stopped under a sign reading "Internet Cafe".

He sat down at the computer and typed in a few letters. Brad's photo appeared on the screen. "This is my son Brad," he said pointing to the screen. He's created his own website. Anyone, sitting anywhere in the world can look at the same picture we're looking at right now.

"What is a website?" asked Nandi.

"Does anyone here know about the Internet?" asked Bill. They all shook their heads.

"We'll you're going to enjoy this," he enthused. "You know how you can phone anyone in the world and speak to them, provided you know their phone number?"

They nodded.

"Well you can visit any computer in the world provided you know its unique address. We've just visited my son's web page. But you could just as easily visit any shop, hotel, factory, university or even a soccer team from this computer. Using the Internet you can find information on anything you want. You can even buy and sell things on the Internet."

They looked at him blankly.

He nodded understandingly. "OK. Let me rather show you how it works. Doris, If I offered to take you to America right now, where would you want to go?"

"I guess I'd want to see the company's head office."

"Why don't we go there now." Bill began typing in an address. They waited for the information to appear on the screen.

"This is Branded Apparel's head office in America." Bill pointed to the screen as the group crowded around. He showed them the photographs of the top management team, the different factories they had around the world, the range of Branded Apparel clothing and the on-line ordering facility.

"Why aren't we on this site?" demanded Jay. "All their other factories are represented here!"

"That's a good point," Bill responded thoughtfully. "We'd better do something about it."

"Go back to the clothes," demanded Rosalie. Bill clicked on the shortcut. She scanned the options. "I want to see the designer clothes." Bill clicked the mouse. "Now I want to see the designers," she demanded.

"Which designer are you interested in? Italian, French, American...?"

Rosalie grabbed the mouse out of Bill's hands. "Which button do I click to make a choice?" was all she asked as she sat down. "Wow this is amazing! Look here, I've found Giorgio Armani's home page."

"I think we've lost her," commented Vuse as Rosalie clicked urgently from page to page.

Bill laughed. "We won't be able to get Rosalie back for a while. We'd better move to another machine."

"Well Mr Library," Bill winked at Vuse. "What articles would you like to read in the world's largest library?"

Vuse thought for a moment. "Let's see what the Internet has on psychology."

"I'm going to ask this search engine AltaVista to search for all the websites dealing with psychology," Bill explained as he put in a search.

A few minutes later Bill showed Vuse the search results. "It came up with 1,52 million websites. Let me show you how you can refine your search and find exactly what you need." Bill handed the mouse to Vuse. Within minutes, Vuse was lost to the world.

"What about me?" demanded Sipho. "I want to find out about the soccer World Cup."

"Sure thing," Bill replied, moving towards another computer. Bill typed in a search.

"What do you want to see – World Cup soccer, women and the World Cup, the World Cup history or the 2002 games in Yokohama?" he asked.

Sipho grabbed the mouse from Bill and sat down in awe.

Nandi wanted to shop on the net. Koos surfed the websites on farming and agriculture, whilst Jay discovered a whole new world of music.

"Anyone want a cup of coffee?" offered Bill. There was no response. Bill grinned and ordered a cup for himself. He sat at the bar watching them feverishly clicking on their mice. Every now and then the silence would be punctuated with a shriek of delight.

Bill stared out of the window, wondering what to do while he waited. He thought he saw Jannie peering in. But when he looked again, there was no one there.

Three hours later Bill looked at his watch. "It's time to go" he announced. The web surfers ignored him. He sighed. He got up and tapped each team member on the shoulder. "It's time to go," he insisted.

"But we just got here," complained Jay.

"No you haven't. It's five O'clock. You've been surfing for three hours now."

Doris jumped up in a panic. "Oh no! If I don't get going now, I'm going to miss my taxi home." "Me too," said Nandi.

"Thank you Bill. That was great. See you tomorrow," shouted Rosalie as she rushed out of the shop.

The next morning, Sipho, Vuse and Nandi were already in Bill's office when he arrived at work.

"I was so excited by this Internet thing, that I couldn't sleep all night," declared Sipho.

Doris waddled in. "Why aren't we on the company website?" she demanded.

"Yes why aren't we?" Jay, Rosalie and Koos joined the animated discussion.

"Can we get an Internet for our factory?"

"We should create our own Branded Apparel website."

"What would we put on the site?"

"What about our factory, our team, and our own range of clothing?"

"We could get our customers to order on-line."

"We could sell clothes from Africa to the whole world"

"And can we order from suppliers from anywhere in the world too?"

Jay voiced their excitement: "I feel I've just entered a whole new world. A world I knew nothing about. There is so much we could do. I can see us having a website for our factory. Customers around the world will be able to order our unique South African clothing on-line. We'll be able to scour the world for new materials, and order from our suppliers with a simple click of the mouse. It is amazing how many opportunities there are for us on this Internet…"

Nandi's eyes were flashing as she spoke: "What I find amazing is how every time we bunk work, we come up with so many incredible new ideas!"

Bill contradicted her. "But you were working when you were surfing the net."

"It didn't feel like work," insisted Nandi. "It felt like fun."

"That's because we're learning new things," said Doris.

"And because we were looking at sites we were interested in, like soccer," grinned Sipho.

Nandi couldn't resist teasing Sipho. "Oh Sipho you're

such a child. You're always excited by anything to do with soccer."

Sipho was beaming. "Me, a child? I'll take that as a compliment. Remember what the sangoma said. It's time to discover our inner child. And you should thank me. How many new ideas did we get at the Bafana Bafana match?"

Koos was thoughtful. "So that's the secret of creativity," he murmured. "If we want to come up with innovative ideas we need to expose ourselves to different environments where we can learn new things. We need to feel like we're playing rather than working. And we must love what we do. I guess creativity is about being a child again. It was just as the card says. When the inner child is satisfied, it rewards you with creativity."

Vuse looked thoughtful. "We're learning so much as a team right now. And we're coming up with so many wonderfully creative ideas. Don't you think we should record our ideas somewhere, before we forget them?"

Jay pulled out his cellphone and began dialling. "I'm going to order a giant-sized white-board for our factory and... excuse me..." he spoke into the phone. "It will arrive this afternoon," he said triumphantly, putting the phone back into his pocket…

"OK," Bill took over the leadership reins, "Can I ask everyone to put down the ideas they like best onto the board this evening. When you get more ideas jot them down so we don't lose them. We'll continue the weekly outings, and in a few weeks we'll choose the best ideas to implement in our factory."

A month later Bill studied the whiteboard urgently, wondering which idea to choose. That morning he'd received a surprise phone call from the director of operations at Branded Apparel.

Peter Hoskins had been quite direct. "I can see you've transformed the factory in South Africa," he said. "The numbers look great. But you need to be aware of the discussions we're having at head office. We've taken a strategic decision to reduce the number of factories operating globally. Within six months we intend choosing five regional centres of excellence around the world. The other nine factories will be closed down. A team from head office will visit South Africa within the next three months to assess your operation."

Which of these ideas would ensure that their factory was chosen as one of the five centres of excellence? he wondered. His eye caught an eye-catching design for "Ubuntu clothing." Could this work? The idea had come from Rosalie after Doris had taken the team to the Lesedi Cultural Village. They'd walked amongst traditional Zulu, Pedi and Xhosa kraals. When Bill had expressed his amazement about the designs on the huts, Rosalie had suggested they incorporate them in a range of clothing. Ubuntu Clothing was born.

What about the eagle, soaring above a rainbow entitled "Rainbow Clothing for the Rainbow People?" Vuse had come up with that idea after Jay had taken them to see the eagles at Roodeplaat Nature Reserve. It had been a special sunny day. A brief thundershower had created a colourful rainbow in the sky. The group had been overawed by the spectacular vision of the eagle flying against the backdrop of the rainbow.

Then there was a picture of bright yellow sunflowers. The group had discussed how flowers grew in nature after visiting Koos' family farm. They'd come up with the idea, that Branded Apparel was like a sunflower. Sunflowers required water, sunshine and soil nutrients to grow. Similarly the people at Branded Apparel needed fresh ideas, personal energy and supportive friendships to flourish. The picture was entitled 'Ubuntu at Work'.

The picture he liked the best was of a child waking up with a yawn, superimposed on a map of Africa. Could this idea be the one? They'd created the idea after Rosalie had taken them to an art museum. Koos had been entranced by a Leonardo da Vinci. When Rosalie explained the concept of the Renaissance, Vuse became quite animated. He spoke with passion about Thabo Mbeki's vision of the African Renaissance, and how they at Branded Apparel should contribute to this worthy vision. That night, Koos had looked up the word 'Renaissance' in a dictionary. The next day he drew the picture entitled 'The Awakening of the Child.' The subtitle was 'The Rebirth and Renewal of Our Company, our Country and Our Continent.'

Bill felt desperate. All the ideas were good. But they needed something more to capture the imagination of the people from head office. Unless they were chosen as one of the five centres of excellence, everything they'd achieved so far would be worthless.

That night he and Vuse discussed their predicament over a beer in Bill's office.

"I'm worried," admitted Bill. We've been playing around like children for a month. And the process has been good for staff morale and for productivity. The ideas have been good too – but..." he sighed, not knowing how to put his feelings into words.

"This is me you're talking to," admonished Vuse, "be honest with me."

"In less than 11 weeks, a team is coming from head office to assess our factory. They'll also be looking at factories in Malaysia, Mauritius, Mexico, London, Chicago and nine others around the world. They're going to choose the five best factories to operate as centres of excellence. The rest will be shut down."

Vuse stared wordlessly at Bill. The implications of their factory not being selected, filled him with dread.

Bill rambled on. "We still can't compete on productivity. Our labour costs are just too high. And we can't simply show off our whiteboard of ideas to the team from head office. They'll laugh at us. We have to think of one big idea that will assure us a place in the big five. And we need to have it up and running before the people from head office arrive. If we don't..."

Vuse interrupted him firmly. "We will, we will."

Bill looked at his diary. "Damn! I have a meeting first thing tomorrow with Woolworths that I can't get out of."

Vuse put his hand on Bill's shoulders. "Relax. I'll speak to the team while you're away. Then we can talk about what to do when you get back."

"Life is strange," Bill thought as he left Woolworths the next morning. For six months now he would have done anything to get Branded Apparel clothing into Woolworths stores. But now, an order from Woolworths simply filled him with frustration. He couldn't focus on his customers now while the factory's survival lay in the balance.

They were all in his office waiting for him. They stopped talking as he entered. As he sat down, Vuse rose and cleared his throat. "We've spoken about our predicament and we've come to a conclusion." He paused, wondering how to say what he had to say, without hurting Bill. "Bill, no offence to you. You are a wonderful leader. But we want to do this ourselves."

Sipho interjected. "You know how you said we need an African solution..."

Jay interrupted Sipho. "Bill, you're an American. If this factory closes down, you'll simply go home to America. We are South Africans. Our jobs and our lives depend on this factory. We want to work with our people to come up with a concept that will impress your head office. Something that shows off our African light to the world. This we need to do alone."

Doris tried to reassure Bill: "We're asking you to give us three weeks, and then we'll present our concept to you. We want you to judge our work through American eyes, as though you were the one choosing the factories of excellence. If you like what we do, then your head office will like it too. And if you don't, we'll still have time to do it your way."

Bill looked unsure.

"We're going to have to ask you to trust us," Vuse pleaded.

"But what are you going to do?" insisted Bill.

"We're going to do like the sangoma says," replied Vuse enigmatically. "We're going to tell our own story."

A week later Bill struggled with his emotions. He remembered Vuse's words. "You're going to have to trust us." "Trust," he mused. Such an easy word to say, and so difficult to practice. He did trust his team. They were a motivated, talented bunch of people. Of course he believed in them. But what if they didn't perform? What if they produced something that he knew would be ridiculed by head office? The people from head office could be brutal. What if they crushed his team? How could he protect them? But if he had to admit it to himself, his real concern was in giving up control during such a critical stage, and he also felt a little hurt about being excluded from all the excitement.

They were obviously keeping things from him. He'd hear their excited voices from his office, but whenever he approached them, they'd hide what they were doing and greet him cheerfully. Once as he returned from a meeting he heard someone shout "Shhh, he's back." By the time he had climbed the stairs, they were all concentrating on their work. But their naughty schoolboy faces suggested they were hiding something from him. One day he arrived at work an hour early. As he climbed the stairs he was surprised to hear choir music emanating from the factory. "What is going on?" he wondered. Like a thief, he tiptoed up the stairs and peered in.

Bill's mouth dropped in amazement. He'd never seen Jay dance or sing before. Yet, in the centre of the room, a jiving Jay was conducting a choir of twenty staff members, singing in harmony. He felt the hairs on his arm prickling. The melody they were singing touched something in his soul. He'd never heard anything quite so beautiful before.

Next to them, Nandi was demonstrating some dance steps to a group of attractive men and women. His eyes scanned the factory. He barely recognised a serious looking Sipho who was showing off samples of brightly coloured materials to Rosalie.

Not wanting to ruin their surprise, he tiptoed downstairs and walked to the coffee shop on the corner. He stayed there sipping coffee until 8.30 a.m. When he returned to the factory, a playful Sipho was hustling Doris with his wheelbarrow, whilst Jay was back to his serious self. Everything looked so normal. He wondered if the choir and the dancing had been a dream.

Bill picked up the paperwork on his desk. There was another order from Woolworths. He smiled as he thought of how much they'd achieved since those days when Woolworths would have nothing to do with them. He casually opened the next envelope. His face flushed with anger as he read the threatening letter from Jannie. He couldn't believe that he was demanding R500,000 in retrenchment fees. He knew he was going to have to confront Jannie But he needed some legal help. Who could he ask? he wondered. Suddenly he thought of Jay and all of his contacts. He called Jay into the office and showed him the letter.

Jay smiled contemptuously at Jannie's cheek. "Don't worry about this," he assured Bill. "I'll get a labour lawyer to deal with it."

He hurried out of the office. Bill cautiously picked up the next envelope. The professionally printed invitation read:

You are cordially invited to attend the dress rehearsal of our launch of a vibrant new range of clothing from Branded Apparel South Africa
Time: Saturday 8th June, 2 p.m.
Venue: Branded Apparel factory, Doornfontein
Dress: South African

At 1.40 p.m., clad in jeans and his South African T-shirt, an apprehensive Bill strolled towards the factory. 200 metres from the entrance he stepped onto the carpet of red crinkle paper, and gazed at the mirage in front of him. The red carpet was lined by flowering pot plants filled with scented roses. Almost in a trance, he followed the inviting music up the stairs where he was greeted by an attractive woman. Thandi was wearing jeans and a shimmering yellow ochre coloured T-shirt that took his breath away. It was covered in traditional Sotho designs. But there was more to it than that. It seemed to resonate a cheeky energy. He wondered who had designed it. Thandi grinned as she led him past the stage, to his front row seat by the modelling ramp.

A buddha-faced black woman in the seat next to him greeted him with a warm smile.

Bill held out his hand in greeting. "Hello, my name is Bill. I haven't seen you here before? Do you work here?" he asked.

She smiled mysteriously. "You haven't seen me, but I have seen you."

Bill looked confused.

"Vuse has come to see me many times on your behalf," she explained. "We are very proud of you. You are doing good things for our people."

"You're the sangoma!" he exclaimed with delight.

She simply nodded.

He tried to speak. There was so much he wanted to ask her. There was so much he wanted to tell her. But the words would not form in his mouth. She took his hand, and a sense of calm enveloped him.

She pointed out two tall young men seated in the front row on the other side of the ramp. "I see you've managed to get some Bafana Bafana players to support you," she commented.'

Bill wondered at Sipho's contacts.

The sangoma winked at him. "You have quite a crowd

here today. You must be very proud." He looked around at the audience. The CEO from Woolworths waved at him. So did the HR director of Fedics. All his clients were here too. How had his people managed to get so many clients to attend a dress rehearsal? he wondered.

The lights dimmed. In the background someone began tapping a drum. The audience took their seats. The drumbeat became louder and more urgent. As it reached a crescendo, Jay strode onto the stage. He held up his hand, and there was silence.

"We welcome you to our factory today. Thank you for taking the time to attend. In three weeks time our head office will be choosing a few factories to become regional centres of excellence. Today's play is a dress rehearsal for a presentation we'll be giving to our head office. We would appreciate any feedback from you on how to improve our presentation. Our future depends on it. And now, I'd like to introduce you to our narrator Vuse, who will tell you our story."

Vuse stood in the shadows at the left side of the stage.

"It was 1998. All was not well at Branded Apparel."

As he spoke three men and three women wafted sullenly around the stage. They began arguing. "Why should I do this?"

"Why should I work overtime?"

"The company doesn't care about us, so why should I care about the company?"

A customer walked on stage and demanded: "Where is my order?"

"Why is your work so shoddy?"

The group simply shrugged their shoulders and ignored him.

The narrator continued: "Apartheid was dead, yet it remained in our souls. Our customers left us. We were alone in our misery."

A man carrying an American flag and a woman carrying a South African flag ambled onto the stage.

Vuse continued: "Then later in 1998, two sangomas came to show us the way. They directed us to a path filled with ubuntu, energy, music and colour. They gave us a dream."

As he spoke a choir led by Doris took the stage. Doris' wonderful voice filled the factory and sent shivers down Bill's spine. Then the choir joined her:

Our clothes reflect our lives
We aim to strip away the clothes of apartheid
And create the clothes for the rainbow nation,
We clothe the nation.
We clothe the world.
We clothe the rainbow people of the world
People with soul. People with ubuntu.
We put soul into our clothes
Our sportsmen wear our sporting range.
Mandela wears our ubuntu range
The world wears our rainbow range.
Clothed in our special energy
Our heroes emerge successful from the battle.

The choir moved off stage. Sipho, Koos, and Nandi

stood in the centre of the stage waiting for the applause to die down. They began asking each other questions.

"What should we do with this dream?"

"How do we make it happen?"

"What clothes would our heroes wear?"

"I don't know, let's ask Rosalie?"

"Let's ask our heroes."

Rosalie walked onto the stage with a clipboard and began drawing to Sipho's instructions. Koos and Nandi pretended to interview a queue of people who streamed across the stage. As each person passed them they shouted out their names. "Bafana Bafana, Nelson Mandela, Woolworths, Yvonne Chaka Chaka." All the while Rosalie drew design after design and tossed these to Sipho. Jay rushed across the stage carrying reams of materials to Doris who was sitting at her sewing machine. Kwaito music drowned out their voices as the lights dimmed. The stage descended into darkness.

Vuse strode onto the empty stage carrying a microphone: "Ladies and Gentlemen, I'd now like to present you with the Branded Apparel range of clothing. Firstly our sports range."

Two members of the Bafana Bafana team jogged onto the stage to the delight of the crowd. Dressed in a range of black and gold shorts, shirts and tracksuits, they stretched, jogged and pretended to kick for goal. The crowd cheered as they ran off the stage.

The haunting music of Doris's choir filled the room.

A man wearing a Nelson Mandela mask jumped onto

the stage. Dressed in a loose-fitting cotton shirt, with a Venda design, he strutted down the ramp saying, "I really like this shirt. I think I will wear it to the opening of parliament".

The audience laughed as he exited.

"And what will our youth be wearing?" asked Vuse. "Soul clothing of course." Nandi led a team of dancers onto the stage. Dressed in an array of shimmering, vibrant clothes that matched their energy, the troupe jived to the beat of Kwaito music. A number of people in the audience stood up, and began dancing in the aisles.

The room became quiet. The stage was empty. Vuse waited dramatically before he signalled to the wings. A group of lethargic people dressed in grey trudged across the gloomy stage as Vuse announced. "From the dark days of apartheid to the rainbow nation."

With shouts and laughter, the dancers leaped onto the bright stage. Doris began singing as they showed off their colourful clothing.

Vuse continued: "As we have transformed ourselves, so we need to share our miracle with the world."

As he spoke, every member of the factory walked onto the stage, wearing a rainbow of different colours.

The audience began applauding. But Doris' magnificent voice silenced them. She sang alone.

As he heard the words, images of Bill's own personal journey of transformation floated across his mind.

The rest of the choir began singing in harmony. The tempo increased. The singing became more joyful.

We uncovered our ubuntu
We discovered our energy
We found ourselves
We are brilliant, gorgeous, talented and fabulous
We are children of South Africa
We are children of the universe
We shine our light on the world.

Vuse spoke into the microphone. "Ladies and gentlemen. I'd like to present to you

Our Ubuntu range,

Our World Cup range

Our Leader range

And our Rainbow range.

But more importantly, I'd like to introduce you to the rainbow people of Branded Apparel."

He pointed to the 80 people on stage. "We have been through an incredible transformation. The energy and the colour that you see in our new ranges, came out of our own transformation. This is the light we want to share with the rest of the world. Thank you."

The choir began to sing the refrain of the Branded Apparel song. The audience rose and joined in. Soon everyone was singing and dancing together. It reminded Bill of the energy at the soccer match, when Bafana Bafana had scored their goal. A spirit of exuberance, excitement and triumph.

Jay took the microphone: "That is the end of our show. But we'd like to say thank you to those that made it possible. Firstly to our leader Bill, who showed us the way. Please stand up."

Bill rose to the applause from the audience.

"Then to our friends from Bafana Bafana. To Unispin, who provided us with the magnificent materials used in our clothes. And thank you to Internet Cafe who designed a website for us for free. That's right, everyone. If you want to see the Branded Apparel range again, or order our clothes on line, go to the Internet Cafe and check out our website at www.ubuntuclothes.co.za. Koos is handing out cards with that address on it. And of course, thank you to all the staff of Branded Apparel, who worked night and day to create this show. We are so proud of you all. Thank you."

Bill tried in vain to push past the excited crowd to congratulate Vuse. But he couldn't even get close to the team. He felt someone tapping his shoulder. It was the CEO of Woolworths. "Congratulations Bill. I've been blown away by what I've seen today. We want all your ranges for our stores both here in South Africa and around the world. We also want to talk to you about exclusivity..."

"Hold on a minute." The CEO of Edgars barged in. "Don't even think of doing an exclusivity agreement with anyone but us. Bill we want as much as you can supply..."

"Excuse me," a muscular man interrupted. Bill couldn't believe his ears as he said: "I would like to talk to you about producing shirts for Bafana Bafana."

It took Bill ten minutes before he could get close to Vuse. "Well done!" he exclaimed. "If you can do the same presentation for head office, we'll definitely be chosen. Besides that, all I can say is that I am so proud of you all." Vuse pumped his hand in return. No words were necessary.

The party continued until well into the night. A tired, but elated Bill finally left the building. His team would carry on celebrating. They had more than proven themselves to him. They had impressed Edgars and Woolworths. They had even got an order from Bafana Bafana. They had won over South Africa. Now they simply had to show their American head office what they could do.

"This is the most wonderful night of my life," he thought as he stumbled on the broken curb. "Nothing can ever take this feeling of triumph away from me."

Not even the grey BMW he saw speeding away out of the corner of his eye.

8 *Touching the Tiger*

What doesn't kill me
makes me stronger

— Albert Camus

A persistent ringing interrupted Bill's dreams. He and Vuse were about to receive an award from Nelson Mandela, when his cellphone went off. He tried to ignore it, but it began to disturb the ceremony. 'You'd better answer it', the president said kindly.

Reluctantly Bill rolled over groping for the phone. He forced opened one eye. The clock read Monday 5.30 a.m. 'Who could be phoning at this time?' he wondered.

Vuse's words washed the remnants of sleep away: "The factory has been burnt down. The police suspect arson. You'd better come in right away."

"I'm on my way now," shouted Bill. He jumped out of bed and raced to the bathroom.

Bill stared incomprehensibly at the black devastation that had once been the Branded Apparel factory. A pile of smouldering rubble, a few buckled window frames and mountains of soot was all that remained of their glorious dream.

He watched as Doris, Jay, Vuse, Nandi, Sipho, Rosalie and Koos, scavenged through the soot, attempting to salvage anything of value. As Sipho held up the charred handle from his yellow cart, Bill saw a tear form in the corner of his eye.

Rosalie put her arm around his shoulders. "All my designs are gone too," she murmured. Fingering a blackened piece of pottery, Nandi whispered in disbelief: "My poor roses. My poor roses."

Koos sneezed as he lifted a small piece of whiteboard out of the rubble. He wiped his hand over it and commented on the irony: "Out of all our ideas, the only one that survived the fire is the eagle flying over the rainbow. But the rainbow is now just soot."

Vuse caught sight of Bill and hurried over. "There is something you'd better have a look at." He led Bill to the blackened steel structure that used to be Bill's office. Bill thought nostalgically of all the evenings he and Vuse had spent together in this very room, and now it was all gone. Vuse interrupted his reverie. "The firemen suspect the fire was started with this," he said, pointing to a grey jerry can in the corner of the room. They stood silently together, staring at the cause of all their misery.

Sipho spotted Bill and rushed over. The rest of the team followed him. A torrent of disappointment, hurt and confusion poured out of their mouths.

"Everything has gone with the fire!" exclaimed Doris.

"After all we've been through, why did this have to happen to us now?" Sipho lamented.

"The firemen asked us if we had any enemies," Koos informed Bill. "But I couldn't think of anyone who would do such a terrible thing!"

Bill thought of Jannie's letter. 'Could Jannie have done this?' he wondered. It was possible, he thought. But the image of the grey BMW speeding away from the factory haunted him. He told the group about his suspicions.

"So Jannie couldn't destroy us as people, so he burnt down our factory," sneered Nandi.

"Jannie wouldn't do this," insisted Rosalie.

Nandi turned to Rosalie. "Why are you taking Jannie's side? You know he's always hated everything we did. He hated us blacks. He couldn't cope if we were more successful than him..."

Bill moved between them. "Hold on," he demanded, trying to smooth out the conflict before it began to bubble. "We can't really prove he did it."

Vuse eyes widened. "Oh shit!" he exclaimed. "Shit! Shit! Shit!" He kicked the jerry can in rage. It tumbled along the floor raising a cloud of soot in the air, and stopped with a clang against the blackened wall. The group stared wide-mouthed at Vuse. They'd never seen their gentle giant lose his temper before.

Then suddenly the storm subsided and the Vuse they knew was apologising to them. "I'm sorry Bill. I'm so sorry everyone. I should have known something like this was going to happen. I should have done something to prevent it."

"What is going on?" demanded Doris. "You have to

tell us. We're in this too."

Vuse took a deep breath and began to explain: "You know Bill's cards?" They nodded expectantly. "There are people who want his cards."

The group stared at Vuse in disbelief.

"Why would anyone risk their lives to steal these cards?" asked Sipho.

Vuse explained slowly: "Bill's cards contain a type of power that everyone wants. The power to transform lives. To understand this, we need to think about the difference the cards have made in our own lives. Remember how we were when Jannie was our boss?"

Sipho pulled up his nose in disgust, and they all laughed.

"Then remember how Bill came to us with his special cards and things started changing. We started changing. We began working together and we discovered our ubuntu. And then we began using that ubuntu to transform our factory."

They listened intently.

"Do you remember how difficult our transformation was at times? How we struggled to find ourselves? How we got depressed? And how sometimes we felt completely lost?" They nodded. They remembered the pain.

"And whenever we didn't know what to do, a card would come to Bill, to show us the way forward?"

"They were very useful," agreed Jay.

"They were more than useful," declared Vuse. "They contained a magic that even our sangoma respected.

Through their words, we were able to overcome all our obstacles. We were able to radiate a spirit of caring in our team, in our factory, and in our clothes. That is what made us so successful. There are a lot of people who would also like to be successful like us."

"And a lot of people who obviously don't want us to be successful," observed Jay.

Rosalie asked the obvious question: "So why don't they just buy another set of cards?"

"Because they can't. There is only one pack of these cards in the world."

"What? How can that be?" demanded Koos.

Vuse continued his story: "In 1994, the president of South Africa expressed an interest in some transformation cards that he'd heard about. He asked his staff to arrange a meeting with the author of these cards. The consultant never made it to the meeting. They found his abandoned car a week later. Neither the consultant nor the cards were ever heard of again – until Bill arrived, and you know the rest."

"Bill, is that true?" Rosalie asked.

"I'm afraid it is," he answered.

"Shit!" they exclaimed in unison. They looked around at one another and laughed. "So they can't stop our transformation by stealing our sangoma cards, so they burn down our factory," observed Koos cynically.

"I guess so."

"What do we now?" asked Sipho.

Bill's answer didn't reassure them: "I don't know. This

couldn't have happened at a worse time for us. After Saturday's show, we had a chance of being selected as one of the five regional centres of excellence. But now, when head office hears about the fire, they won't even waste their time visiting us. They'll shut us down immediately."

"But what will happen to us?"

"What will happen to our families if we lose our jobs?"

"What will happen to our staff?"

"How can we tell them that after all they've achieved, they're going to lose their jobs?"

Bill couldn't answer them. He turned away and stared at the piece of whiteboard that had once reflected their dreams. He thought of all they'd been through together. How they'd overcome their distrust. How they'd worked through their pain and their anger. How they'd discovered their inner child. How they'd created a factory filled with ubuntu, energy, hope and music. And how on Saturday they'd been the brilliant, gorgeous, talented and fabulous children of the universe. He looked at each of them in turn. Doris, Jay, Nandi, Sipho, Koos, Vuse and Rosalie. It was so unfair. This wonderful team had lost far more than a factory in the fire. They'd lost their jobs. They'd lost themselves. And they'd lost their glorious future.

"Excuse me," Koos was grinning as he spoke. "Doesn't head office prefer solutions to problems?"

Bill nodded. How often had he heard that refrain?

"So?" asked Bill.

"So what if we created our own solution, before we get

them all concerned about the fire."

"Are you saying what I think you are saying?" asked an incredulous Bill.

Vuse put his arm around Koos. "Koos my man, when you're good, you're good. We're going to give a message to those that started the fire. Our enemies may have burnt down our factory, but they haven't destroyed us. We still have our spirit. We still have ourselves. We can rebuild this factory."

"If we could survive apartheid, we can survive a fire." Doris held up her fist as she spoke. "We are still going to shine our light on the world. And it will be a brighter light than ever before."

Bill was bursting with pride as he shook everyone's hand. "OK everyone, I guess I will forget to mention the fire to head office. But we have only seven weeks till the visit. What is your plan Koos?"

The ever pragmatic Koos spoke clearly and directly. "The first thing we have to do is to find out exactly what was lost in the fire. I'm going to need everyone to help me with this. I want to know what equipment and materials were lost in the fire, what jobs we were working on, and what our new ranges consisted of."

He began directing: "Doris and Vuse, the staff will be here in half an hour. You need to reassure them that they still have their jobs. Find a place to work. Then I need you to find out the following information: what equipment were they working with? What equipment do we need to replace? What jobs were they working on in the weeks preceding the fire? And finally, find out how each of them contributed to our new ranges, and then pass this information on to Rosalie and Sipho."

"Rosalie and Sipho, we need you to recreate the ranges you developed for our show. Begin by putting together a list of all the clothes in each range. Then ensure you have the designs for each item in each of our new ranges. Before you redesign everything, see if any designs survived the fire - maybe you were working on some at home Rosalie? Maybe you have some copies of your designs left? Maybe some of them are on our website?"

"Jay, go to the Internet Cafe. Print out all the designs and photographs on our website for Rosalie. I also need you to find out whether the factory was insured. Put in a claim and find out how long it will take to pay out. Also Jay, can you talk to our suppliers? We need to reorder all the materials we were working on to fulfil both our existing client orders, and the materials we used to create our range for the show. You'll need to get information from Rosalie and Sipho for the new ranges, and from Doris and Vuse for customer orders."

"Bill and Vuse, you're to go and see each of our clients. Find out what orders we were working on for them. But also ask them for help. We're going to need new premises for our factory. Maybe they have an unused warehouse we could move into. We're going to need sewing machines, interlockers, and furniture. Maybe you can barter with them. Items from our new range of clothing in payment for premises..."

Koos pointed to the coffee shop on the corner. "We'll meet at the Coffee Pot tomorrow at 8 O'clock. Get as much information as you can in the meantime. Nandi, I need you to work with me on the master plan. We are going to recreate not only our factory, but also the spirit that drove it."

At 8 O'clock sharp, Bill pushed open the door to the Coffee Pot. It felt warm and cosy. The team were already seated at a table, warming their hands around steaming cappuccinos. As Bill moved towards them, he breathed in the aroma of freshly ground coffee. He stopped, remembering a coffee shop on a different continent, in a different life. He recalled the steam rising from his cup as he'd wondered if he'd ever find a job again after Papas. He remembered how he'd been led that day to the Dickensian bookstore, and how the card *You deserve more* had fallen from the dusty green book on the top shelf. He smiled at the parallels. Even today, he and his team did deserve more. But this time, things were different. This time they were going to get the support they deserved. He bounded over to the table and gave a delighted Koos a high-five handshake.

"We are back in business," he announced with a broad grin. "Where is my coffee?"

"First you tell us your news, then we decide if you deserve your coffee," teased Sipho.

"Edgars has an empty building we can move into tomorrow." Bill grabbed the coffee from Sipho. He continued with a self-satisfied look on his face. "They are centralising their warehouses and haven't disposed of this property yet. We don't even have to pay rent for three months – providing they get an order for our complete range of Ubuntu clothes for their Christmas sales. And, the CEO of Edgars insists that we come to him first if Branded Apparel even thinks of closing us down."

Bill took a big sip of coffee and waited for the applause.

"Okay, you deserve your coffee," conceded Sipho playfully.

"And that's not all," continued Vuse. "Mr Price can get us eight old sewing machines to use until we get sorted out."

He signalled the waitress: "I'll have a coffee now please," he declared smugly.

"I've already had my two cups of coffee," boasted Jay with a wink in his eye. "Unispin have agreed to give us all the materials we need by the end of this week. And we only have to pay them in three months time. I need to get our order in by tomorrow. Koos, I need to know the quantities we need." Koos nodded. Jay continued. "I've already printed out Rosalie's designs, plus all the photographs of the finished garments from our website."

"I don't think I can drink as much coffee as I deserve," declared Doris proudly. "One of the members of my church group has her own factory which makes safety clothing for companies. She is going to bring us three sewing machines and one interlocking machine. And four of her people are going to help us for a month. All she wants in return is for Rosalie to do a few designs for her. She wants to branch out and begin making business uniforms. Can you do some designs for her Rosalie?"

"Sure," Rosalie smiled. "But she is going to have to wait. We've managed to find thirty-five of my designs. But I still need to recreate another ten designs. I will try to get them done by Friday. And I'm going to bring in my sewing machine from home. An extra machine should help..."

Nandi jumped up. "What are we waiting for then? Let's go see our new premises."

"You go ahead and sort out things from that end," smiled Bill. "Koos, Vuse and I are going to do some detailed planning. In seven weeks time, we are going to show the people from head office something they will never forget!"

It was a typical Gauteng winters day. A biting cold numbed Bill's hands as he drove to the new Branded Apparel factory in Sunninghill. Although he and his team had worked until 3.30 a.m., he still felt pumped up. He arrived to find his eighty brilliant, gorgeous, talented and fabulous children of the universe stomping their feet outside a large white warehouse. As the doors to their new factory, their new lives, opened, they rushed in from the cold.

The large empty storeroom felt empty. The eighty heroes gazed in disappointment at the dingy grey walls of their new home. Bill moved to the centre of the room. "It's not exactly cheerful...?" His voice echoed in the void.

Jay sprang towards Bill. "But then our old factory under Jannie wasn't that great either, was it?"

"Not until we put the ubuntu into it," shouted Doris.

"And music," sang Jay as he turned on his ghetto-blaster. Nandi began dancing to the kwaito beat.

The group began to relax.

"This place needs some colour," declared Sipho. "Yebo Sipho. We want to see your yellow wheelbarrow," called large Lydia. "OK, OK, I'll make another one" grumbled a delighted Sipho. "But only if Nandi brings in some more pot plants. I need something to dodge around." Nandi stuck out her tongue at Sipho.

"I need some help with this wallpaper," Koos pulled the elastic bands off a roll of flipchart paper.

"Cheap looking wallpaper," grumbled Mark the packer.

"Where must they go?" called Lydia, grabbing a large sheet.

"It's been used before," Lydia pointed to the pencilled sketches and scribbles on the page.

"Don't worry about that for now," instructed Koos, "Let's just get them up."

"Wait!" shouted Rosalie. "They have to be put up in order. Look at the numbers on the back of each page. Sipho, help us here."

Sipho grabbed bundles of Prestik and strode to the far left-hand corner of the factory.

"Who has number one?" yelled Sipho. "Look at the back of your page. We need number one here."

"Number two goes here," instructed Rosalie.

"Where is number three? Come on guys, we have a whole room to cover."

Each member of the factory grabbed a flipchart page and began to fall in line.

They were so focused on getting the papers onto the wall in the right order, that they barely noticed the mural that was being created. Finally the last page was stuck onto the wall. They stepped back to look at their work. A crowd of grey lifeless people faced the radiant children of the universe. Lydia pointed at the sketches on the wall. "Who are these people?" she demanded.

Vuse stepped out in front of the mural and smiled. "These are the grey people of our world, who need a touch of rainbow colour from us," he declared.

Lydia's eyes sparkled. "Like in our play?" she asked.

"Yes, just like in our play. Koos will explain how we're going to bring these people to life."

Koos stood in front of flipchart number one. "Ok everyone. Come closer so you can read the writing over here." They crowded around him. "What we have on these walls are sketches of every item of clothing we need to produce before head office comes to inspect our factory. If you look closer, you'll see some pencilled writing on each sketch. These are the detailed specs for each item. For example over here I've detailed the material that needs to be used, the quantity we require, the machines to be used, the project team to work on this item, the project leader, and the targeted date for completion. So the first project is to fulfil the Woolworth's order. Doris is the team leader. Lydia, Jacob, Susanne and Alfred will work with her for the next six days. The second project is the entire Ubuntu range. Jay is the project leader. Johannes, Piet, Marius, Paul and Sarah will work on the Ubuntu range for the next 10 days. Now if you look at the rest of the pages you'll see other projects. Your project leader will tell you what to do.

Sipho pointed to the cans of paint standing in the centre of the front wall. "Don't forget to tell them about the paint," insisted Sipho.

"And now for the part that Sipho likes best," smiled Koos. "Once your team has completed a project, let us know by painting in the relevant sketch on our mural."

"The paints and brushes will be left here," shouted Sipho.

"And," Vuse remarked softly, "when these dull grey people are transformed into a mural of rainbow children, we will be ready to share our light with the world."

The next seven weeks passed in a blur of compressed images for Bill. He noticed the factory becoming more and more crowded. Bill would look around and recognise people, but he didn't know where they were from. One day he counted the people in the factory. One hundred and fifteen. Branded Apparel only employed eighty people. Where had the rest come from? He counted the number of sewing machines. Twenty-five. They'd only had twelve machines the last time he'd looked. He was puzzled.

He'd finally asked Doris: "Who are these people, and

where did all these machines come from?"

Doris had given him that look that suggested he should already know the answer to his question: "That lady over there is Sipho's sister. She's taken a day off work to help us. And she brought in her own sewing machine. That is Rosalie's younger brother packing over there. Vuse's sisters are working with Jay over there."

Bill thought he recognised the tall dark man who was racing around with Sipho's yellow wheelbarrow. "Who is that?" he asked.

"Oh Bill, how can you even ask me that! That is Benni McCarthy from Bafana Bafana. He and Sipho were at school together. About 20 of Sipho's schoolmates have been here to lend a hand. And over there is the sangoma – you do remember her don't you?"

Bill approached the smiling black Buddha. Before he could say a word, the sangoma grabbed his hand.

"Ah Bill, you've got quite a turnout again. You must be proud," she declared.

"To be quite honest, I'm totally puzzled," replied Bill. I don't know who half these people are, and why they are all helping us."

She smiled mysteriously. "What you're experiencing is the real spirit of ubuntu."

Bill looked at the magical scene being played out in front of him. To the sounds of kwaito music hundreds of elf-like spirits were cutting, sewing, and packing garments in fast forward motion. The sketches of lifeless people were being transformed page by page into a vibrant mural of colour.

A large black cauldron bubbled in the centre of the room. "What is that?" asked Bill thinking he'd been transported into some kind of fairyland.

"That," laughed the sangoma, "is potjiekos. Koos' wife has been cooking that for hours. The people must be fed you know. It is 9 O'clock after all."

Bill felt embarrassed. Unlike the sangoma he found it difficult to recognise where the magic ended and reality took over. The sangoma began to move towards the potjiekos.

"Wait," shouted Bill. "There is something that's been worrying me."

"Yes?" she asked gently.

"Well, you know my American sangoma cards?" She nodded. "Whenever we've had a setback before, a card has appeared to show us the way."

"Yes?"

"Well this time, there has been no card at all. And we haven't seemed to need it either."

As she gazed at Bill, a current of positive energy encircled his heart. "You did get a card." She said. She pointed to her large bosom. "Your card is here."

Bill looked perplexed. "You want me to write it out for you?" she asked with hint of a smile. Bill found himself nodding. She found a piece of paper and carefully folded it into a small card. She took out a pen and wrote a few words. She handed him his gift. On the paper she'd written:

The hero you seek is you

A delighted Bill read the card. "Yeah!" he exclaimed. "We are the heroes. Me, the team, our factory and this group... so that's why..."

She interrupted him: "I think the food is ready now." She shuffled to where Koos was dishing out his potjiekos. Bill could swear she was laughing at his sudden insight.

The tape depicting the heroes' achievements played in double speed. The pictures on the wall were coloured in one by one until a colourful wall of rainbow colours surrounded the factory. Each day completed orders were shipped to their clients. Each day more people came to show their support. Sports stars, television personalities, members of parliament, singers, businessmen and their customers. All of them wanted to be part of the story of Branded Apparel's triumph over adversity.

The people from head office had come and gone. They had been there to witness the last clothes coming off the production line. They'd asked about the story behind the colourful mural, and had listened in amazement as Nandi explained the concept of ubuntu to them. They had commented on the energy that had seemed to be radiating from the people and the clothes of Branded Apparel. They were there when the newspapers wrote about Branded Apparel and its amazing transformation:

'Ubuntu Thrives Over Adversity'; 'Why you can't burn a rainbow', 'Branded Apparel — shining the light of ubuntu' were some of the headlines that impressed them the most. The photograph of Nelson Mandela wearing a Branded Apparel shirt particularly delighted the Americans. As Sipho explained to them, one of the parliamentarians who had attended their launch had told the president about Branded Apparel's transformation. He'd loved their range of clothing for 'rainbow people' and had immediately ordered five shirts.

It seemed like everyone wanted to be part of the Branded Apparel miracle. Orders for their new range of clothing flooded in. From South Africa. From Africa. From Europe and from Asia. Everyone wanted to own a garment imbued with energy. Bill, Vuse and Jay could barely respond to all the calls for interviews. Let alone the requests for them to talk on the secret of transformation at various conferences.

Sipho described it simply: "Branded Apparel had suddenly become internationally cool."

They'd summoned Bill to attend a meeting at head office with the operations director Damon Ackerman. He'd taken the plane from Johannesburg to New York, and from there on to Atlanta.

While waiting for his connecting flight at JFK, he'd become aware of someone watching him. He turned around and there she was, staring at him in amazement. He felt overwhelmed by a torrent of conflicting emotions. He hesitated, uncertain as to whether or not he should approach her. She walked confidently towards him.

"Bill. Is it really you? What a coincidence! What are you doing here? You look terrific," Sharon gushed.

"So do you," he responded carefully.

"I've got half an hour before my connecting flight. Do you have time for a cup of coffee?"

Drinking plastic coffee in a plastic fast food outlet, they'd chatted about Brad, her career and their friends.

Then she asked him about Africa. As he spoke about his adventures she listened intently and then remarked: "Africa has changed you. You look like the Bill I married 16 years ago. You've got your fire back. But there is something else. You've discovered a strength, an inner wisdom."

His response was interrupted by the airport announcement. "They're calling my plane. I must go." She handed him her card. "Look us up when you have some time. We've been missing you." And she was gone. He wondered if it had all been a dream.

He sat in the reception area of Branded Apparel head office waiting for the moment of truth. In half an hour's time he would know if everything they had achieved in Africa was enough. Either they were going to become a centre of excellence or they were going to be shut down. Either they had a bright future ahead of them or it was all over. It was strange. He didn't feel anxious at all. Sharon was right. No matter what head office decided, he had changed. They had changed. They all had an inner wisdom now. They had their transformation cards. They had their spirit. They had their special energy. It didn't matter what head office decided. They could overcome anything.

Damon Ackerman led him into the empty wood panelled boardroom. He offered Bill some coffee. Then he came directly to the point.

"We're very impressed by what you've achieved in Africa. We were blown away by the success of the ubuntu and rainbow ranges in South Africa. We are thinking of launching these brands globally. We were also impressed by the way you turned around the South African factory. Do you think you could perform the same magic on our other factories? We have a challenge for you. You have one month to come up with a strategic plan to bring this special energy to our factories around the world."

9 Sitting on the Back of a Chained Tiger

If you try to possess it
you will destroy it

— Tao

"Why aren't you happy?" asked Vuse. "We achieved everything we wanted, didn't we?"

"We sure did." Bill hoped he sounded more positive than he felt.

Around Bill, eighty people were laughing, crying, hugging, and shaking one another's hands in celebration.

"We did it. We did it!"

"We saved our factory!"

"We did more than that; we're going global my man!"

"Africa is now going to show the rest of the world how to do things."

Bill slipped away from the crowd as Doris led the factory in a triumphant rendition of their song. Alone in his office, Bill tried to figure out why he was feeling so depressed.

Vuse knocked softly on the door. "Something is obviously worrying you." He shut the door and sat down facing Bill. "What is it?" he asked gently.

"I don't know. I think I'm concerned about this strategic plan we have to submit… " Bill hesitated, "I'm not sure we can do it."

A hint of a smile crossed Vuse's eyes. "What do you mean, you're not sure we can do it. Aren't we the fabulous children of the Universe?"

"That's just it," sighed Bill. "Up to now it feels as though we've just been children playing games in a small country somewhere in Africa. Now we're moving into the real world of international business. I'm not sure we've got what it takes to develop the strategic plan head office has asked for."

Vuse stared out the window, lost in thought. Finally he spoke: "You've been climbing a mountain together with a team of eighty South Africans. It was a difficult climb. You reach the summit, tired but elated. While your team looks down at what they've achieved, you look up – only to see another peak in the distance."

"So they celebrate while I wallow in depression," Bill sighed.

"The problem is, I just don't know how to tackle this thing. I've developed loads of strategic plans in my time. But this is different. This is far more complex."

"Talk to me. Sometimes by speaking things aloud, we clarify our own thinking," offered Vuse.

"We have to do three things simultaneously. One, we have to develop our rainbow and ubuntu ranges into global brands; two, we have to train people in factories around the world how to produce these brands; but three, the most difficult requirement, is that we have to instil the special energy we have created into all these factories. The Branded Apparel operations manager asked if we could perform the same magic on our other factories!"

As Vuse nodded encouragingly, the words began to flow out of Bill: "It's difficult to explain the magic in our clothes to others. You see, what makes our clothes so attractive is that they radiate energy. That energy is derived from the spirit of our people. It is the spirit of caring, which has been imbued into the fabric of our clothes, that creates the magic."

Vuse reflected Bill's concern: "What you're saying is that if the workers in the factory around the world don't have the right energy, the clothes they produce will be lifeless. They'll be like the figures around the walls of our factory, before we painted them in rainbow colours."

"Exactly!"

"Hmmm... "

Deep in thought, they sat side by side gazing out of the window. Overhead a flock of birds floated by. A motor scooter jumped a red robot. A taxi hooted, then skidded to a stop. Five large ladies heaved themselves and their parcels into the minibus. Nonchalantly, a street child kicked a stone. He bent down and rubbed his foot in pain.

A distant memory of a flash of purple under a brick swept through Bill's mind.

"We need a sangoma card!" he thought.

"What would the sangoma say?" wondered Vuse.

An image of the sangoma filled Vuse's being. He imagined her sitting in her darkened hut, in front of him. A few bones lay scattered on the mud floor. She swayed, as if in a trance. Vuse felt dizzy. He felt her words echoing though his throat.

To meet the challenge
you have to know
how to accomplish
the impossible

The image dissolved. Vuse slowly opened his eyes. Bill was staring curiously at him.

"I don't know where that came from," Vuse admitted. "But I was imagining what the sangoma would say to us right now. And these words came into my mind. Any idea what they mean?"

Bill looked at Vuse's drained face. "I think we have our new card," he observed gravely.

They stared at one another in delight.

"Have you ever accomplished the impossible, Vuse?" Bill asked flippantly.

"I don't think so," replied Vuse.

Bill waited.

"Hold on, that's not true," exclaimed Vuse. "I once thought that it was impossible to work together with management, and now look at us: going global together!"

"What about you?" he challenged Bill.

Bill smiled at the memory that floated into his mind.

"When I first took over here, the most impossible challenge facing me was to get you lot to stop toy-toying long enough to produce 500 T-shirts for Fedics."

They both laughed, recognising how far they'd come since those days.

"Maybe we do know how to accomplish the impossible," remarked Vuse.

"Maybe we already know everything we need to know," pondered Bill.

The door burst open. Sipho peered in. "We wondered where you'd got to. You've been missing all the celebrations." He looked at their serious faces. "What's up?" he asked cautiously.

"We were just listing all the impossible things we've accomplished at Branded Apparel," explained Vuse.

Sipho pulled a chair towards him and sat down. Doris, Jay, Nandi, Koos and Rosalie followed him in.

"Have you got down how we got Nelson Mandela to wear our clothes?" Sipho offered.

"What about being chosen as one of the five centres of excellence," suggested Doris.

"Rebuilding our factory after the fire," proposed Koos.

"Capturing the energy from the Bafana Bafana match into a range of clothing. Do you remember how you challenged me at the soccer match, Bill?" asked Rosalie. "I thought you were joking at first – but then Sipho and I started thinking about how we could do it..."

"Wait," Doris stood up to emphasise her point. "Do you know what our biggest achievement was?" She demanded. Her eyes rested on each of them in turn. "It was learning to trust one another." She hesitated for a moment then continued. "Do you remember how we had to clean away the apartheid in our hearts, in order to release our ubuntu? To me that was our most painful experience and our biggest achievement."

"Our biggest achievement, and our biggest lesson," agreed Koos solemnly.

"What lesson, Koos?" asked Vuse gently.

Everyone went silent. An embarrassed Koos hesitated before he replied. "There were so many lessons. But for me the most painful one was realising that I'd become used to carrying a burden of anger and bitterness around with me. It wasn't easy taking the load off my back and placing it on the ground in front of me. I had to summon up the courage to open the bag, and face the demons that had been hiding there for years. Only then could I see them for what they were. Powerless ghosts of my past. They begged me not to leave them behind. They said I wouldn't be able to cope without them. It took a lot of faith to walk on and let go of my past."

"Me too," agreed Doris. They all nodded in sympathy.

Sipho waved a flaming torch to ward off the descending gloom. "I learnt how soccer can be used to help business," he declared.

Nandi jumped up. "I learned it was OK to play."

"I've learned that play is the secret source of creativity," added Koos.

"I learned to believe in myself," Rosalie asserted.

A philosophical Jay commented: "I learned we could make music together."

Before Jay could continue, Sipho's tapping feet had provided the beat. A gentle melody from Doris was enough to get Nandi up and dancing. "That's just what I mean," laughed Jay. "Before Bill arrived, I didn't trust people who were different from me. I didn't realise that it's our differences that make us special. And when we apply our differences to a worthy goal, we create music together. For example, I didn't know that Rosalie was a genius designer. Sipho introduced colour and fun into the factory. I brought in music – as well as supplies."

He smiled. "Our master of logistics, Koos ensured we covered all the bases. Doris and Vuse motivated the staff and got the job done when it mattered. Nandi infused our people with energy. And Bill showed us that it was okay to be ourselves."

"And when we are true to ourselves, we discover we have a special light that we can share with the world," added Vuse.

"And what did you learn Bill?" Asked Nandi cheekily.

Bill hesitated. "Like Koos, I've learned so much in the last few months. But my biggest learning was that as a leader I don't have to know everything. I also don't have to be in control. When I'm lost, I've learnt to trust that something, a magic card, a sangoma, or a voice will come along to show me the way."

"I can't believe we forgot about the American sangoma cards," declared Vuse. They were such an important part of our transformation. People even burnt down our factory to get hold of them. We are going to need their lessons to help us to instil ubuntu into the other Branded Apparel factories around the world. Bill, won't you recite each card to us again?"

Bill obliged.

1) Every day nature paints her sunset, with or without you.
2) It doesn't matter whether it's fair or not.
3) You deserve more.
4) Let go and the world will come to you.
5) Polish away the grime to reveal the shine.
6) Satisfy the inner child first.
7) The hero you seek is you.
8) To meet the challenge, you have to know how to accomplish the impossible.

They sat in silence, colouring the wisdom of the cards with their own personal experiences. A hooting taxi brought them back to the present.

Bill commented, "Now I understand what the last card means. We have proven that we can accomplish the impossible. We've also learned many lessons along the way. We now need to apply the lessons we've learnt to our new challenge."

He paused. "Are you ready for the next mountain we're going to climb?"

"Sure thing!" Nandi's enthusiasm was echoed by the group.

Bill continued. "Our new challenge involves achieving

three goals: One, we need to develop the Rainbow and Ubuntu ranges into global brands; two, we need to train people in factories around the world to produce these brands; and three, we need to inject our special energy into all the people who produce our clothing. We need to develop a strategic plan regarding how we're going to do all of this by the end of the month. Any ideas on where to start?"

"Yes. I have an idea." Pragmatic Koos took the lead. "Why don't we follow the same steps we used to develop our Ubuntu and Rainbow ranges. That was a type of strategic plan, you know. For example our first step involved collecting creative ideas from many different sources."

Sipho's eyes lit up. "We could ask the management of Bafana Bafana," he exclaimed. "I have a contact there..."

"Oh Sipho, to you everything is about soccer." Nandi rolled her eyes.

A hurt Sipho retorted: "Bafana Bafana have international experience you know. They are a global brand. We could learn something from them."

"We could indeed," agreed Bill. "Woolworths is also a global brand. We could learn from our customers too."

"And when it comes to instilling ubuntu into the factories, we could get some advice from our sangoma," added Vuse. "And from our own people," admonished Doris. "They've also had experience you know."

"So," Koos began writing on the whiteboard:

1) Get creative input from different sources

"And then," Jay continued, "we developed our play. Remember the scene where the grey people of the world, were replaced by energetic dancers in rainbow colours. We basically acted out a scene of our future success, as though it were occurring today."

"Then after the fire," Bill continued, "we created a detailed plan using a 'paint by numbers' wallpaper. By looking at it, anyone could see 'who had to do what, by when, according to what standards."

"Don't forget the best part," added Sipho. "Whenever we'd achieved a milestone, we painted over the grey people. At any stage we could see how far we'd got towards achieving our dream."

"So, let's summarise." Koos read aloud the points he'd listed on the whiteboard:

1) Get creative input from different sources.
2) Create a vision of the future, as though it were occurring today.
3) Detail who must do what, by when, according to what standards.
4) Create a self-monitoring system to measure progress.

"That's it!" Koos was satisfied that he had something tangible to work with. "Let's get going people." He grabbed a clipboard and began organising.

Exactly one month later, the plan was couriered off to head office. The waiting began. Bill was proud of what they'd produced. The plan contained all the usual components of a strategic plan such as branding, design, production, quality control, marketing, distribution, finance, technology and human resources. But in addition, they'd developed some really innovative ideas.

Bill thought particularly of the mission, logo and vision they'd developed:

Our mission: To help people discover what is special within them through either wearing our clothes or being part of our rainbow universe."

Our logo: A torch shining a light of rainbow colours with the slogan – colour your life with our rainbow light

Our vision: To send ambassadors of transformation, diversity and creativity to every Branded Apparel factory. The ambassador will use the eight steps of transformation to release the positive energy within every factory worker. This energy would then be reflected in the clothes they produce.

While they were waiting for a response from head office, Executive Conferences approached them to speak at a conference on transformation. At first Bill had refused, but Eric Moyo had persuaded him that the Branded Apparel success story contained a message of inspiration and hope that people in other companies needed to hear.

"You see," he pleaded, "people have lost their way. To

many organisations, transformation is about embracing new technologies, following best practices, cutting costs, retrenching people and restructuring. The people, however, find that they are getting hurt by 'transformation.' Many have responded by bailing out of corporations and going in search of 'personal meaning'. I've been hearing so many companies complain about how difficult it is to retain good people. I believe it's because companies have forgotten how to care. In our quest for profits, we've taken the heart out of our organisations. That's what makes the Branded Apparel success story so important. Your message on how to put the soul back into business is something you simply have to share."

How could they refuse such an impassioned plea? Before long, twenty thousand pamphlets were sent to 8,000 organisations around the country. Bill and Vuse's photographs appeared next to these words:

> *Don't miss the presentation on the Branded Apparel success story. Bill and Vuse will share with us their eight secret steps to transformation.*

On the day before the conference, FedEx delivered an 'urgent' letter to Bill. Looking at the handwriting on the envelope, Bill commented to Vuse: "It's great to receive something still written by hand in this electronic age." He tore open the envelope and took out the letter.

"What is it?" asked Vuse, noticing the colour draining from Bill's face. Bill handed him the offending page. It contained numerous adverts for funeral parlours. At the bottom of the page, the words: *Don't talk at the conference, unless you've planned well ahead,* were scrawled in red ink.

"If this is some kind of joke, I don't think it's particularly funny." Bill was obviously irritated.

Vuse smiled grimly. "I think we're now becoming a threat."

"To who? The people who burnt down our factory?" asked Bill.

"Whoever didn't want us to succeed in our own transformation, obviously doesn't want us to share what we've learned with the world. I think we should take this threat seriously," suggested Vuse.

"Are you suggesting we don't speak at the conference tomorrow?" asked Bill defiantly.

"I just think we need to consider the risk," responded Vuse calmly.

Bill stood up and strode around the room. "Damn the risk," he shouted. "Damn the risk! The conference organisers said we had an important message to share with the world. This stupid threat just confirms how important our message is. I think we've got to do it – no matter what the consequences."

"OK, I'm with you on this!" The comrades in arms gave each other a high-five handshake.

"Okay, Let's do it. But we need to be prepared. What if whoever is threatening us tries to kill us at the conference? How do we ensure our message still goes out to those that need it?"

"We need to get our message out to the world before the conference." Agreed Vuse. "What tool can we use to achieve that?" He pondered.

They both shouted out the answer simultaneously. "The Internet."

"We need someone we can trust to post it on the net."

"It' s 6 p.m. We need someone who is prepared to work through the night."

"Or someone in another time zone."

"Brad!" they both shouted in delight.

"No problemo" was Brad's reply. "E-mail me the stuff you want on the site, and leave it to me."

Night and day, on both sides of the world, they worked feverishly at their computers.

Finally at 2.40 a.m., Brad phoned to say the work was done. They logged onto their website, and there in glorious rainbow colour, complete with graphics, were the eight secrets of transformation.

"I have one last concern about tomorrow," admitted Bill. What if the people who are threatening us are at the conference. What if they learn the secret of transformation from us, and then use it for evil purposes.

Vuse answered softly. "What those threatening us don't understand is that the real secret of transformation is not something that can be understood. It has to be experienced. It is not about knowing. It is about doing and becoming. Transformation cannot be bought or stolen. It can only be achieved through personal experience. And that requires trust, faith, energy, perseverance and patience. Those who are seeking instant knowledge will never experience transformation. We have achieved enough tonight. It is time to rest."

Bill and Vuse slept soundly.

At 10.15 a.m. the next morning, Bill and Vuse entered the crowded conference room. Eric spotted them. He shoved his way through the crowds.

"We have the most amazing turnout," he shouted. "There isn't even standing room left. Follow me." He began pushing. "Coming through!" he warned.

"Ladies and Gentlemen. We are privileged to have with us today, two extraordinary people, from an extraordinary company. Branded Apparel. You've all read about the success of the Ubuntu and Rainbow range of clothing. Now to tell you about the secret behind their success, I present to you, Bill and Vuse." Eric left the stage.

Looking down from the stage at the mass of humanity in front of him, Bill felt the adrenaline pumping through his body. He spotted Jerry in the front row, looking stressed.

"We didn't know how important our message of transformation was, until we saw the large turnout here today. Thank you for being here," Vuse announced to tremendous applause. "You should know that we were warned not to talk at this conference. Someone didn't want our message to be shared at all. The eight secrets of transformation that you're going to hear about today are now available around the world at www.rainbowenergy.com. If you forget this address, it's linked to all the search engines on the topic of change, transformation or energy. And now Bill, a special American/South African will talk to you about the Branded Apparel story."

As Bill spoke, a wave of positive energy swept through the room. People were nodding their heads in agreement, applauding Branded Apparel's successes and taking numerous notes. An hour later Eric had to stop the questions and beg the delegates to go to lunch. In the dining room, Vuse and Bill were constantly surrounded by well wishers whose comments reflected how the Branded Apparel story had touched their lives.

"Thank you for giving us hope."

"I'll be buying all your clothes."

"Wearing the rainbow shirts will remind us of our ubuntu, our humanity and our spirit."

"Finally I understand what I've been grappling with for so long... "

"You inspired me today. I'm now going to do something that I've been too scared to do. I'm going to follow my dream."

Eric guided Bill and Vuse to the speaker's table. "I think our speakers deserve some lunch," he announced to the throng of well-wishers. "You've created quite a ground-swell today," remarked Eric. "Maybe we should talk about future events."

"Let's have some lunch first," said Vuse. "Suddenly I feel quite hungry."

"Ah, Mr. Bill". Bill looked up from his smoked salmon starter to see a jovial Jerry Khumalo.

"I've come to say goodbye," Jerry boomed. "I see you are finally going back to the United States."

The diners laughed uneasily at Jerry's attempt at a joke.

"I'm not going anywhere," countered Bill. "The Rainbow Nation is my home now. So I guess you'll just have to put up with me." He smiled at his fellow diners. They voiced their approval.

"I'm afraid we are going to have to lose you, after all." Jerry's confident smile unsettled Bill. "This brand you've created is too important to stay in a small African country. I wish you well." He shook Bill's hand and strode away, waving to the crowd as he went.

"What's he up to now?" Bill whispered to Vuse.

"Damned if I know," responded Vuse.

Back at the factory, Bill received an urgent message to phone Damon Ackerman at head office.

"I need you in New York next week Thursday," he ordered.

"What's it about?" asked Bill.

"We're having a strategic planning workshop for the new African range."

The spark of doubt lit by Jerry ignited into a raging fire.

"You're talking about the Ubuntu and Rainbow range? But we've developed a strategic plan for that already."

"With all due respect, Bill. This is too important a project to be led by sangomas and local people. This range deserves the best of everything." Bill didn't like the condescending tone in Damon's voice.

"We've managed to get Matt Goodwin, the world's best

strategy consultant to facilitate our strategy session. A number of top designers, retailers, and merchandisers will also be attending. It's been quite a coup. Make sure you're in by Thursday. I'll email you the details!"

From the moment Bill landed at JFK, he felt depressed. Compared to South Africa, New York seemed devoid of colour. The winter clouds blocked out the sun, making the buildings look drab. Unsmiling drones hastened past him on the sidewalks. And the people. They were polite. They were efficient. They were focused. They were friendly. But they were different. It was as though they were stripped of sunlight outside and inside their beings.

The strategy session was frustrating. Bill watched as the so-called experts droned on about how brilliant and important they were. They hadn't taken the time to look at any garments from the Ubuntu or Rainbow ranges. They hadn't even bothered to read his strategic plan. They didn't care about the magic behind the new ranges. They weren't interested in injecting the spirit of ubuntu into their factories. All they were interested in was merchandising, design, production, and profits. Especially profits. He felt betrayed by their greedy self-interest.

The marketing director noticed Bill's lack of involvement in the discussions and cautioned him not to 'be so negative'. Bill needed to 'lose his ego' and 'become a team player.' Bill tried to be enthusiastic. But he was filled with a sense of dread that he couldn't quite articulate. When he looked at the 'experts' around the room, they reminded him of the people on the wallpaper of their factory in South Africa. Grey, lifeless figures who didn't even know they needed to be touched by rainbow colour.

After three days of deliberation, the professionals came out with a strategic plan for 'The Fire in You' and 'Colour Your Life' ranges of clothing. John Galliano from the House of Christian Dior agreed to fix the design. Saatchi and Saatchi would handle the global advertising campaign. Manufacturing would be done in Malaysia, Thailand, Mauritius and South Africa under the auspices of Damon Ackerman. Bill would move back to head office as an assistant to Damon. He was expected to be ready to begin his new role within two weeks.

The grey weather followed him to South Africa. Unseasonable storms caused his plane to be diverted to Durban. When he finally arrived at the airport, he ignored the chatter of the other passengers as he waited impatiently for his baggage. He found himself being irritated by the children playing near the baggage carousel. "Pardon me," he hissed, as he pushed past a 'curly-topped angel' to get to his bag. He didn't have time to waste. His sole focus was on getting out of the airport.

He dreaded telling them the news. How could he explain to his team that all their work had been in vain? That their strategic plan had been ignored? That the Ubuntu and Rainbow ranges were now called 'The Fire in You' and 'Colour Your Life' series? That profitability and professionalism would drive the new strategy? That there was no room in the plan for ubuntu, transformation, energy or creativity?

How could he tell them that their glorious dream had been hijacked by a soulless team of 'professionals' who had stripped their vision of all its colour and radiance? How could he say that after surviving criminals, muggings and fires their dream would finally die of corporatisation? He laughed cynically as he opened the door to his home.

He slept fitfully. He dreamed he was back at Papas. They were retrenching him. He'd sold his health, his family and his life to the corporation, and they were now throwing him out. But it wasn't Papas. It was Damon Ackerman. It was the people at Branded Apparel. They had tossed Vuse, Doris, Rosalie, Jay, Koos and Sipho into a muddy bog. His team couldn't swim. One by one they sank below the mud. They shouted at him to save them, but he couldn't. He was chained to a tree. He pulled at the chains in frustration. But he was trapped. Jerry, the people from Papas, and the lawyers were laughing at his distress. Suddenly through the mist, he saw Rose. She was begging him to fight. He called to her. She dissolved. Sharon stood in her place. Brad appeared beside his mother: "Fight them Dad!" he screamed. "You can fight them, you know." Then he was gone and Bill was all alone. He began to panic, tugging desperately at the chains.

Looking up at the sky, he noticed it had turned red. A bright yellow thunderbolt hurtled towards him, thudding into the ground. In front of him stood the sangoma. She calmly pointed to the chains at his feet. On her forehead were written the words 'Stand Tall.' He tried to stand up, but his hands were chained to his feet. He was a baby tiger. He woke up whimpering.

He went to the bathroom and drank some water. 'What was that dream all about?' he wondered. Then he saw the pattern. It was Papas happening all over again. He created the magic. They destroyed it with bureaucracy, professionalism and experts. He helplessly went along with their plans. When they failed, he got blamed.

"Well, it isn't going to happen to me this time," he resolved. This time the dream would end differently. He sank back into a deep sleep.

10 Releasing the Chains

Talk with a free heart and
your message will be true

"Our conference presentation seems to have had quite an effect on people. I've left all the fan mail on your desk for you to read." Vuse shook Bill's hand warmly as Bill entered the factory. "Welcome back. How was New York? How did the strategy workshop go?"

"Not so good. We all need to get together to discuss what happened. Can you organise a meeting in about two hours time and... " Bill acted on a whim, "can you ask the sangoma to be there too?"

Vuse raised his eyebrows. Bill shrugged his shoulders as if to say: "I don't know why I asked, but let's just trust this feeling, shall we?"

He sat down at his desk and began reading. Each letter strengthened his earlier resolve.

"Thank you for giving us hope," he read.

"People say that the only way to get meaning at work, is to leave the corporate world."

"You've proved that companies can still provide a

sense of purpose."

"Thanks to you we're going to try to make our company more humane."

Spotting the sangoma talking quietly to Vuse, Bill rose to greet her.

"Thank you once again, for being here to help us." He led her into his office while Vuse went in search of the rest of the team.

"You have a difficult choice to make," she said simply.

"I do," responded Bill.

It seemed to Bill that she was looking inside his very soul. They sat in silence until the rest of the team arrived.

Bill decided not to soften the blow: "The strategy session didn't go well for us at all," he announced. "They decided to use John Galliano from the House of Christian Dior to revamp all our designs." He noted Rosalie's dismay and moved on. "Our ranges will now be known as 'The Fire in You' and 'Colour Your Life' series. While the clothes will be manufactured in Malaysia, Thailand, Mauritius and South Africa, head office will control everything. The focus of the new range will be on production and profit streams. There is no room for creativity, transformation or personal development in the new ranges."

No one said a word. They stared at him in shock, not quite believing that head office could betray them so. Bill delivered the final blow: "Oh, and I've been recalled to New York. I'm to report there for duty within two weeks."

They gasped in dismay.

"But you can't!"

"They can't... "

"Not now. Not after all we've been through together."

"We can't lose you now!"

"What will happen to us?"

"Is this what you want?"

They all turned to look at Bill waiting for his answer to either crush or uplift them.

"No. It is not what I want." He spoke with a quiet determination. "After all we've been through together, after all we've learnt, I know I can't go back." He paused. "I will not work in a company that has no soul. I will not work without purpose."

Taking courage from Bill's defiance, Sipho jumped up and proclaimed: "To hell with head office. If they don't want us, we'll do it without them!"

"We'll buy the South African operation," shouted Jay.

"We'll start our own business," asserted Koos. "We've already got everyone supporting us in South Africa. We can go it alone."

"Didn't Edgars say that we should contact them first, if head office didn't choose us as a centre of excellence? Maybe we should go and talk to them," suggested Rosalie.

Bill observed the sangoma contemplating everyone's reactions.

Then Vuse rose. Holding up his hand for silence, he spoke with a quiet authority: "A few weeks ago, we stood up in front of thousands of people and told them that it is possible to experience personal growth and meaning within a company. Since then, we have been overwhelmed by thousands of letters and emails from people who have been touched by our message. Our website is getting 5,000 hits a day. By sharing our story, we have become role models of ubuntu and transformation. Every employee working in a soulless environment, and every grey person seeking to be coloured by our magic, is looking to us to show them the way.

We cannot run away now just because head office has rejected our strategic plan. In the Zulu culture a hero doesn't scamper off like a dog with his tail between his legs, when things don't go his way. He stands up and fights. We too must stand tall. When we go into battle against the forces of bureaucracy, we are fighting not only our own company. We are fighting against every organization that carelessly snuffs out the spirit of its workers. We are fighting to keep alive the hope we've sparked in all those that wrote us letters of appreciation. We are fighting for every customer and every worker who might become a little brighter because of the clothes we create, and the way in which we create them. We are fighting to reclaim the spirit of every person in every factory, in every land. We are fighting for the right to shine our rainbow light upon the world. We cannot run away from our responsibilities."

Chastened by his words, they sat in silence. Finally, Bill spoke hesitantly. "I guess I am going to have to go and speak to the Board of Directors." He sighed deeply, thinking of the battle ahead of him. "Will you come with me Vuse?"

Vuse shook his head sympathetically. "No Bill. I don't understand the American culture. This is something you're going to have to do alone."

It's not going to be easy," Bill sighed. "I don't know what to say to the people at head office. They speak a different language. We speak the language of transformation, trust, meaning and soul. Head office is led by accountants, lawyers, and marketers. They speak the language of market share, ROI and turnover. If I try to explain the concept of ubuntu, or the role that the sangoma cards played in our success, they'll laugh me right out of the boardroom. I know I have to fight this battle, but this is a battle I just don't know how to fight."

They stared at one another. They shook their heads. They shrugged their shoulders. No one said a word.

"What do you think I should do, sangoma?" Bill asked in desperation.

She raised her hand, as if to demand silence. Sitting cross-legged on the floor, she opened her pouch and took out the bones. She mumbled in a low tone, threw the bones, chanted, and then stopped as if to listen. A few minutes later a smile appeared on her lips.

"The answer lies in a dream. Has anyone had any powerful dreams lately?" She asked.

"I have." Bill tried to recall his dream. "The night I returned from America, I dreamt that I was chained to a tree. The people from head office had thrown all of you into a bog. I tried to rescue you, but I couldn't move. My wife, my son, and an American friend begged me to fight. But I was a baby tiger, and my hands were chained to my feet. You," Bill smiled at the sangoma, "you were also in my dream. You had a sign on your forehead which said 'stand tall.'"

"You have your answer," the sangoma whispered.

"I don't think I understand," Bill replied.

The sangoma rose from the floor, and eased herself into a comfortable chair.

"Let me interpret your dream for you then," she offered. "The chains on the tiger represent our desire for control, certainty, ease and honor. It is our fear of losing our chains that keeps us where we are. It takes enormous courage to break out of our chains and release our inner tiger."

Bill shook his head. "I still don't understand," he said.

Bill strained to hear her wisdom.

"When you don't need to be in control, when you don't require certainty, when you thrive on challenges, and you don't need others to respect or honor you, your heart will be free. Talk with a free heart and your message will be true!"

"I understand now," he whispered solemnly. "Thank you. I want to thank you more than I can express."

The sangoma simply nodded her head.

Never before had Bill felt so sure of what he was doing. "I'd like to speak to Neil Johnson, the Chairman of

Branded Apparel," he spoke clearly into the phone.

"The chairman is busy in a meeting," Neil's secretary responded cheerfully. "Can I ask what it's about?"

"This is about whether I and the Ubuntu and Rainbow range of clothing stay within the Branded Apparel fold, or whether we choose to operate independently from South Africa. I would like to have an hour at the next board meeting to present the alternatives to the Board of Directors."

"Please hold on," Bill waited patiently, smiling at the note of anxiety in her voice.

"The chairman says we can fit you into the board meeting next Wednesday. You can have the 4 O'clock slot." She sounded a bit put out.

"Thank you," Bill responded politely.

He replaced the phone, and shouted to himself: "Yes!"

As he packed his bags for New York, he found himself alternating between feelings of anxiety, determination, fear and certainty. Impulsively, he dialled Sharon's number and left a message on her answering machine: "I'm coming to New York on Wednesday to do something I should have done years ago. I'm going to stand up to the Board of Directors of Branded Apparel. Think of me at 4 O'clock!"

They were all at the airport to wish him well. Vuse, Rosalie, Koos, Doris, Jay, Nandi, and all the staff from Branded Apparel took turns to pump his hand and give him messages of encouragement.

"This is for courage." The sangoma pressed a small

bone into his hand.

"What is it?" he asked.

She grinned mischievously. "Let's just say it is the tooth of a tiger."

Suddenly she was gone. Fat Lydia enveloped him in a bear hug and they were calling his flight.

"This is such a different world," Bill thought, as the yellow taxi dodged in and out of the traffic until it finally choked in the motorway gridlock. He looked at the occupants of the cars beside him. The professionally dressed woman in the car next to him glanced impatiently at her watch. The taxi behind him seemed filled with delighted hand waving tourists. 'It is strange', thought Bill. 'Everyone is leading their normal lives, and I am going into battle.'

He casually switched his cellphone on. It beeped. There was a message from Sharon saying "Good luck for the board meeting. We're proud of you."

The taxi driver interrupted him, "Hey, this is where you get off". It was show time.

As he took the lift to the 43rd floor Bill clutched the tiger tooth in his trouser pocket. "Courage," he thought as the doors opened. For an instant, the warrior stood tall. He stepped out into the large imposing room. In the centre of the room was a lonely piece of antique furniture. A stern gatekeeper occupied the mahogany desk. Behind her, wall to floor windows provided a panoramic view of the city.

"How can I help you?" asked the receptionist.

He felt the fear seeping into his stomach.

"I am due to address the board at 4 O'clock. My name is... "

"Please be seated," she interrupted him. "I'll tell them you are here."

She left her fort and disappeared into the adjoining room. Bill heard her announcing his arrival. "Next agenda item... he's here now... "

"They won't be long," she announced. "Please take a seat."

Bill looked around the room. He noted the mahogany furniture, Persian carpets, professional assistants, wall to ceiling windows and of course, the view of New York. "So this is what power is all about," he thought.

A vision of the sangoma floated into his mind. "Not very impressive is it?" She pointed scornfully at the trappings of power. "You have experienced far more power than this!" she chanted as she faded away.

An insight flashed through him. With their creativity, he and his team in Africa had been connected to the infinite power of the universe. The power on display on the 43rd floor of this New York office was limited to a few lifeless symbols of wealth. There was nothing to fear here.

"Welcome to New York, Bill," Bob Gross, the grey suited human resources director greeted Bill cheerfully. "Marvellous job you did in turning around our African operation," he remarked, as he steered Bill towards the boardroom.

The suits around the boardroom table stared dispassionately at him as he entered the room. "Let me introduce you to everyone," offered Bob. As he was being led around the room, Bill tried to make a note of his impressions so he could share them with Vuse on his return.

"This is Tony Fox, our legal director." The 40-year-old, striped navy suit stood up to greet Bill. It seemed to Bill that Tony's head didn't fit correctly onto his body. "Was it good posture that made his neck look so rigid, or had he been in an accident?" Bill wondered.

The first thing Bill noticed about Branded Apparel's financial director was his squeaky voice. It seemed to go with his short stocky frame and his balding head. Paul Green peered disdainfully at Bill from behind his oval glasses.

Bill's new boss stood up to greet him. From his firm handshake to his gravelly voice, everything about Damon Ackerman exuded strength.

Branded Apparel's marketing director, Clara Whitford took herself seriously. Her clothes, her hair and her words were carefully chosen to make a statement. Clara didn't suffer fools easily, and her manner made this absolutely clear.

"And this is our chairman, Neil Johnson," he heard Bob say. About sixty-odd. Grey hair. A pleasant face. He looked more like a kindly uncle than a chairman. Neil Johnson greeted Bill with a twinkle in his eyes. "Welcome Bill. We were very impressed about what you achieved in South Africa. Are you still enjoying it there?"

"Thank you, I am," replied Bill politely. Neil smiled warmly, and invited Bill to sit down.

The chairman opened the discussion: "As you all know, Bill here, is the person responsible for the innovative brands that were developed in our South African operation. Bill asked for some time to address us on the future of these ranges. So, I'd like to welcome him here today. Over to you Bill."

Bill stood up to speak, but his mouth was dry and furry. He felt himself drowning in a bog of panic. Just like in his dream. His mind went blank. He heard Paul cough. Neil poured himself a glass of water. Bill stared at the group in dismay. What was he going to say to them?

He suddenly remembered the sangoma's words:

When you don't need to be in control
When you don't require certainty
When you thrive on challenges,
and you don't need others to respect you,
your heart will be free.
Talk with a free heart and your message will be true.

He smiled and began speaking: "Thank you for giving me the opportunity to address you. Recently, the executive management team presented you with a strategy for Ubuntu and Rainbow brands. Today, I am going to present an alternative, more powerful strategy which was developed by my team in South Africa."

"But," interrupted Damon, "You were in New York last week. You participated in developing the very strategy you are now suggesting we reconsider."

"Yes I was at the workshop last week," conceded Bill. "However, I was very disappointed with the outcome of that workshop. The strategic plan that was finally developed stripped away everything that made our clothing so popular in Africa, and indeed internationally. I am concerned that if we follow the strategy developed in New York, it will be a major flop. Let me explain why."

The brave warrior proceeded to deliver the speech of his life.

"We are living in a high tech Internet age. A world of global competition, flexible workforces, business reengineering, downsizing, rightsizing and constant change. Within this world, people are searching for meaning. Some are leaving corporations to 'find themselves' in their own small businesses. Others leave to join the thousands of dot.com companies that are springing up. Some simply stay in the corporate world, lamenting the demise of 'companies who care.'"

In South Africa, we stumbled on these trends almost by accident. Having come through a period of apartheid or separation of races, South Africa is seen as a miracle in action. Nowhere else in the world has there been a change of government, a change of ideology and a transfer of power on this scale, without a war. Bishop Desmond Tutu termed this miracle 'the rainbow nation'. He spoke with pride about a nation of diverse people, working in harmony to create a powerful new country.

"Our team at Branded Apparel experienced a similar

miracle. By going through a process building trust and discovering what made us special, we were able to come up with an innovative brand that excited people not only in South Africa, but around the world. Our Ubuntu and Rainbow brands." (Bill noticed Paul yawning. Clara winked at Paul as if to say, she too was bored.)

"What makes our brands special is our people. Our workers are filled with a special kind of energy. This is transmitted into the clothes they create. People who wear our clothes feel and respond to this positive energy. This is what has caused so much excitement. This is why everyone from the president of South Africa to our national soccer team wants to wear our brands. This is why the three biggest retail chains in South Africa, have chosen to stock our brands. This very energy is what attracted you at head office to consider developing a brand from South Africa into a global brand. The strategic plan that was presented to you was developed by the world's best designers, retailers, advertisers, and branding experts. There is no doubt that they developed a highly professional plan. But it is a plan stripped of energy, colour and spirit."

"I'm not sure where your speech is leading," said Clara, who could no longer contain her impatience. We have the designs we need already. We don't need all this esoteric stuff. We simply need to produce these designs globally. Let's just get on with it already," she announced looking for approval from the rest of the board.

"Which is more important to you? To simply produce

two new brands, or to have factories around the world that are continually creating exciting new brands? What will you do when people lose interest in the 'Fire Within You' and the 'Colour Your Life' brands? Surely you don't want to lose out on a constant stream of innovation?"

Bill noticed Neil's eyes sparkling. "I'd like to hear your views on innovation, Bill. Please continue."

Reenergized by Neil's interest, the words flowed from Bill's soul.

"The reason companies find it so difficult to innovate is people don't understand the nature of creativity. Creativity is a flash of the divine. When we truly create, universal energy is transmitted through our hearts, into our work, and into the products we create. Our products become imbued with a special type of energy. It is this energy that attracts people to our brands. They buy from us, because through wearing our clothes, they are touched by this universal energy. But you can't package soul in a product if your people have lost their spirit... "

Bill noticed Clara pulling a face at Damon. He winked at her as if to say, 'this is a load of shit.' He looked at Neil. The chairman seemed to be lost in thought.

The warrior made his final stand. "I am fighting for more than just the Ubuntu and Rainbow brands. I am fighting for a style of working together in our factory that enables people to be their best. To be creative. To be true to themselves. I am fighting for my soul, your soul, and the soul that is in the brands we create. The soul that people want to buy... "

"Excuse me," Paul's voice was full of ridicule. "I didn't know we were in the business of saving souls. I thought we were here to make money." Tony laughed in agreement.

Clara and Damon were whispering amongst themselves and laughing at the obvious joke – Bill and his religious zeal.

Bill sat down. "Oh no," he thought in dismay. "I've lost it. I shouldn't have gone on about souls. They didn't buy it. They didn't even understand it."

Neil took control of the meeting. "Thank you Bill. Gentlemen, Clara, we've all heard the impassioned speech from Bill." Bill cringed with embarrassment. He couldn't even look at the other board members. The chairman pointed to the door. "Bill could I ask you to wait outside for 10 minutes please."

Feeling dejected, Bill waited in the empty reception area. 'Should he leave now and save himself further embarrassment?' he wondered. He thought of Vuse, the sangoma and his team. He felt consoled. He had given it his best shot. He had spoken with a free heart. His message had been true. It was now up to them.

Bob came out of the boardroom. "We're ready for you now," he said gently. Bill braced himself for the worst.

"Please sit down," Neil pointed to an empty seat. Bill waited for the ridicule.

The chairman voiced the verdict: "For some time we've been discussing the need to establish an innovations division. It seems while we have been talking, a group of people in a factory in Africa, have claimed that role for themselves. As well as increasing productivity by 200% and profitability by 48%, they have been able to come up with a concept that has delighted customers around the world. We think they should be encouraged to continue. What we would like you and your team in South Africa to do for us Bill, is to establish a centre of innovation. You will be responsible for replicating your way of working in our factories around the world. Each year, we are going to ask you to transform two factories into centres of innovation. Each year we expect the factories you control to come up with ideas of the same calibre as your Ubuntu and Rainbow concepts."

Bill's obvious delight amused Neil. The kindly Chairman pretended to get tough.

"You and your team will have a limited budget to work on. And you will only be kept on as long as you keep producing concepts and returns as you did in South Africa. You will report directly to me. I am particularly interested in learning about the secret of the soul." He winked mischievously. "That's all. The meeting is adjourned."

As the meeting broke up, Neil took Bill aside. "I would like to meet with you tomorrow at 9 O'clock. We have a lot to talk about. I think I'm going to have to visit South Africa, to see what a factory filled with spirit looks like." He grinned. "By the way, I'd like to congratulate you on your courage, young man."

Bill danced out of the boardroom. He hugged an old lady in the lift. Her face lit into a surprised smile. As the doors opened, he raced to a waiting cab. Without thinking, he gave the driver the address of Sharon's apartment building. He pushed the button for the lift. Then he changed his mind and sprinted up the stairs. Brad opened the door.

"Who's there?" called Sharon. She appeared in the doorway. She gasped in delight at the sight of Bill dancing around the room. "What is he doing?" asked an incredulous Brad.

"I've never showed you my John Cleese act, have I Brad?"

Bill laughed.